Time Travel Adventu

BOO

C000148861

Robert P McAuley

Published by Robert P. McAuley

The Premise

The **Time Travel Adventures Of The 1800 Club** is a 21 st Century haven for people seeking to escape New York City's frantic pace. Dressed in clothes their ancestors might have worn during the 1800s, members enjoy foods of the period and read periodicals featuring news of a particular date in the 1800s. However, the **1800 Club** also has an astounding secret . . . *Time Travel*. Members travel back in time nudging famous persons and key events just enough to ensure history unfolds, as it should. Guardians-of-the-past, living in the future, send robotic probes back through the ages, discovered that, at critical time-junctures, pivotal figures stray from vital tasks and actions. These Time Watchers of the past can't go back and fix the glitch in the timeline because the atmosphere they breathe has been cleaned up over the years and the air of the past is almost unbreathable for them. Then an **1800 Club** member from the 2000s are sent back to guarantee that events get back on track. The **1800 Club's** members aid Lincoln, Roosevelt, Bat Masterson, Mark Twain and many others. Without subtle interventions by these unknown agents, the famous might have been only footnotes, rather than giants of history.

Dear reader, I once read a time travel book where the main character went back over one hundred years in the past to retrieve an object from a house. He entered the house, picked up the object and brought it back to his time. To me it was upsetting that he took us back in time and never once said anything about the house! Never described anything! He might as well have just gone back to a park where things never change. That is why I try to bring the reader along with me as I travel through time. RPM

Books 2 through 19 are also available.

Time Travel Adventures of the 1800 Club: Book 1
The Abraham Lincoln Mission

A flash of lightning illuminated the newspaper folded next to a steaming cup of tea on the antique mahogany coffee table. The November 10, 1862 headline screamed in bold type - **LINCOLN FIRES GENERAL MCCELLAN, WAR DRAGS ON!** A slim finger slowly followed the smaller print beneath it.

Yesterday, November 9, 1862, it was announced, to the satisfaction of this newspaper and many others, that Major General George Brinton McClellan was dismissed as Commander of the Union Army. This newspaper wishes to applaud President Lincoln for finally taking such matters to task. It was after the Battle of Antietam that he was ordered to turn over his command to his good friend, General Ambrose E. Burnside and go home to New Jersey to await further orders. We of Harper's Weekly wish much success to General Burnside.

Prescott Stevens, president of the 1800 Club, raised the wick of the oil lamp he was reading by and picked up the TV remote next to his tea. He aimed and clicked it at the big-screen TV opposite him and rubbed his eyes as he went to the Weather Channel's 7:00 P.M. broadcast. After finishing the mid-west coverage, the young woman said, " . . . and in the New York, New Jersey, and in some areas of Connecticut, rains, accompanied by thunderstorms continue for the second straight day. It promises to let up early tomorrow."

Turning the set off, he stood and stretched to his full height of five-feet seven-inches and rubbed his plump stomach. He faced the full-length mirror and buttoned the vest of his three-piece, brown suit then tightened a dark brown silk cravat around his starched collar and pushed the pearl stickpin through and into the shirtfront. Stevens patted his short brown and gray beard and pulled and twisted the almost-full handlebar mustache until he was fairly satisfied. He pressed a button next to the large mahogany desk and was answered immediately by his butler and right-hand person, Matt.

"Yes, sir?"

"Matt, has the weather deterred many of our dinner guests?"

"No, sir. All guests have texted or e-mailed their acceptances."

Prescott nodded and asked, "So, we can expect Mister Bill Scott to attend then?"

"Yes, sir. Mister Scott e-mailed this afternoon that he'd be attending this evening."

"Thank you, Matt. Oh, and Matt, I've just finished proofing the newspaper and it may be distributed for this evening's dinner."

"Very well, sir."

Prescott signed off and sat back down in the large, soft leather easy chair once again and took a sip of his tea.

Less than one hour later a taxi splashed a torrent of water at Bill Scott, who nimbly jumped out of the way only to step into a rain-filled pothole. Shaking what water he could off his shoe he looked across the street at the six-story, brownstone townhouse as he shivered. *I'm going to get soaked by the time I get there.*

Lightning flashed as he ducked under an awning across from his destination at 520 East Ninth Street in New York City.

The rain made the street slippery and seeing an elderly woman slip, Bill used every inch of his 6 foot 2 inch frame to reach her. She grabbed onto his arm as he steadied her and his well-toned muscles gave her the reassurance she needed on such a night.

"Oh, sir. I thank you so much."

"No problem. Are you alright?" She nodded and smiled as his baritone voice simply added to her image of a heroic figure. A passing cab splashed them both and its headlights showed her hero's gray eyes squint in the wet onslaught. Still holding her with one arm they both stepped away from the curb and he pushed back his military style dirty blond hair with his other.

"I'm fine now, sir. And I again thank you."

His broad smile showed an almost square jaw that a movie star would give anything for including the small red scar on his chin. The scar was because he looked up too soon while crawling under barbed wire during his time with the U.S. Navy SEALs. Another result of that incident was his friends ribbing him that they knew when he was under pressure because the scar turned a deep red color.

The team was right and as Bill was about to cross the street he could almost feel the heat the scar seemed to give off when he was under any pressure such as darting out into traffic to help that elderly woman.

It was a night just like this when he told the team he was not going to re-up for another tour.

"What? Why?" they asked in disbelief. He gave them a few stupid excuses, but never the real one: he just could never take a life. He was afraid that because of that he might jeopardize a mission and even the lives of his teammates.

Looking both ways, Bill pulled his overcoat tight and ran between parked cars across the wet street and almost collided with the doorman at 520.

"Evening Mister Scott. Wet one, isn't it?"

"Yeah, Jim, but it could be worse . . . could be snow," Bill answered thinking: *A standard answer for a rainy November evening.*

The doorman held the door open and Bill entered. He went downstairs, sliding his hand along the well-polished, curved mahogany banister, and then walked on the dark brown wall-to-wall carpet. An oversized ornate wooden door with a large brass handle faced him. His cold fingers fumbled for the old-fashioned key each club member used for entry. *This is one of the many things I love about the club: No electronic entry card, no worry about a power failure, a plain and simple old-fashioned and reliable key. This is the way it should be.*

He inserted his key, and the door swung open noiselessly. He went in and smiled as he heard a low hissing sound. *Gaslight,* he thought. *No neon or incandescent lighting making harsh shadows. Just gaslight with its soft yellow flickering glow that makes a person feel safe.* Bill's theory as to why people felt safe around the controlled, dancing gaslight flame was that it had been ingrained in the culture since early mankind discovered that fire kept the danger away. But whatever the reason, it did make him feel more relaxed.

Standing at the end of the hallway was a slim man with thinning, salt and pepper hair parted down the middle. Dressed in dark pants, jacket and shoes, a red vest over a white, heavily starched shirt with a dark bow tie at his neck told Bill that he was one of the club's butlers. However, unknown to Bill was the fact that Matt Worthington came from a long line of butlers who ran some of the largest homes in England over the years and as the job description of 'Butler' was out of date in Europe, it was he who made the 1800 Club tick.

Bill acknowledged him, "Good evening, Matt."

"Good evening, Mr. Scott. May I help you change, sir?"

"No thanks, Matt, but if you could put my coat and shoes somewhere to dry, that'd be great."

"Yes, sir, I'll attend to that straightaway."

Bill nodded. "Do you know what's on the menu tonight?"

"Roast goose, sir, with baked potatoes, glazed carrots, gravy and beets."

Bill smiled, "I'm drooling already. Tell me, is Stan Walker here this evening?"

Matt's eyebrows arched over his blue eyes as he quickly went over the guest list before nodding yes and Bill cringed as he thought, *Oh well, maybe I can avoid him.*

He entered a small walk-in closet that had his name etched in a silver nameplate on the door and sat on an upholstered bench to remove his wet shoes and socks. From the rack he selected a brown, wool three-piece suit, white shirt with a stiff collar, and a brown cravat. He added a mother-of-pearl stickpin and sat to button his brown, high-topped shoes. A final look in the full-length door mirror revealed a six-foot, two-inch dark-haired man from the mid-eighteen hundreds looking back at him.

While many of the club members could trace their family tree back to the 1800s, he could not. He knew that many of them dressed as their ancestors did and when in the club they impersonated them while he had to settle for being an average businessman from the 1800s. *Still,* he thought as he tightened his cravat, *I love the thought of being back in the easier times of the 1800s.*

He opened the door and handed out his damp shoes, socks and overcoat to Matt and after thanking him for his service Bill walked down the mahogany-paneled hallway to another door and pressed a button. A humming sound announced the arriving elevator. The door opened, and a young man in a dark brown uniform topped off with a flat cap greeted him.

"Good evening, Mr. Scott."

"Evening, Drew. Nice size crowd tonight?"

"Not bad, sir. Especially for a rainy evening."

"Good, good."

The door opened on the main floor, and Bill stepped out. He heard the mumble of indistinct voices as he headed to the spacious room filled with other club members. He saw a stack of newspapers on a small, mahogany table just outside the doorway and picked one up and looked at it.

I love it! No e-mail here, he thought as he folded the newspaper, *no Charlene Greene either. Then again, no Charlene Greene out there anymore, either, except of course when I go to work. Boy, I really have to change jobs.* He winced, *Got to stop thinking about her . . . got to, but four years is a long time to hear her suddenly say, "It's not you, it's me." Then asking if I could get a different apartment.* He shook his head; *she seems to have forgotten that she moved in with me four years ago!*

He stood straight and looked in a long mirror. "It's a new life," he said to his reflection. "Each day is a new day and I'm going to have fun doing things I've always wanted to do." He smiled at himself- "Like coming to my club and indulging in my favorite pastime; pretending that I'm back in the mid-eighteen hundreds."

He entered the room and noticed the cigar smoke that clung close to the ceiling. A waiter approached him with glasses of white and red wine. "Wine, sir?"

"Thanks," Bill said, lifting a glass of the red.

He walked over to a window covered by heavy, red, floor-to-ceiling drapes, which were always kept closed. *No sense in making believe that we are back in the mid-eighteen hundreds if we see the present-day New York skyline.* He put down his wineglass and picked up a cigar from one of the silver trays strategically placed around the room and lit it. He blew a large, round oval of smoke and watched it join the haze close to the ceiling.

"Bravo! I tell you, Bill, we should have a smoke-ring contest. I do believe you are the only person who can get close to matching my orbs."

Bill smiled at Philip Corouso, a heavyset, gray-bearded man in his mid-fifties. "Well, Philip," he retorted, "I do believe that you take lessons from those smoke-belching cannons of your artillery unit."

The big man laughed and the medals on the breast of his blue uniform tinkled against each other. The crossed-cannons on his collar denoted that he was a colonel in the Union Army's artillery unit as was his great-great grandfather. "You also have the fastest retort in the club."

Bill nodded graciously.

The colonel continued, "I'm serious. And I don't think I've ever heard you speak out of 'club time.'"

"It's easy for me not to drift out of it, sir, as I've always been happy in 'club time.' And I do believe we are walking a fine line even acknowledging the term 'club time.' Agree?"

"Yep! Right you are," answered the colonel taking a long pull on his cigar.

"I do not wish to be another Stan Walker," Bill said looking around. "I understand he's attending tonight's dinner."

Philip nodded as he exhaled. "Yes. He's still a member. But . . . the word is he's on probation, and nobody will talk to him. Nobody wants to take a chance and slip up if he starts speaking of . . . of . . . err . . . speaking of other things."

Bill winked. "Right."

Phil took a final swig of his drink. "Got to excuse me, Bill. Have to use the facilities, and it's hell with these buttons." He grinned and walked off.

Bill looked around the room at the other members, but he was content to lean against the windowsill and enjoy his cigar, sip his wine and glance at the Harper's Weekly headlines; **LINCOLN FIRES GENERAL MCCLELLAN, WAR DRAGS ON!**

It's easy, he thought, *for me to stay in 'club time' because I'm happy in 'club time.'*

He had long felt that the 1860s must have been a wonderful period, except for the war. But it seemed as though there was a war almost every twenty or thirty years and it came with the territory.

Bill glanced up to see a thin man approaching him. *Darn! It's Stan Walker.*

Too late to escape, Bill smiled and started a conversation along the correct lines.

"Evening, Mister Walker. It seems as though Mister Lincoln fired another general. Pretty soon we'll have no one left to lead our boys to victory. What say you of this latest turn of events, sir?"

Walker fidgeted with his cravat, obviously uneasy with it. "Uh . . . yes . . . I . . . err . . . I haven't seen tonight's paper. He fired McClennon you say?"

"*McClellan*, Mr. Walker, not McClennon. General George *McClellan*. They say he was inept. Kept letting the Johnny Rebs slip away."

"Oh McClellan. Yes, I remember now. He lost a few battles, didn't he?"

"More than a few, sir."

"So, Mister Scott. How do you think the war will turn out?"

"Hard to tell, Mr. Walker. We northerners have the railroads and that's a big thing in our favor."

"Yes, and if I remember my history correctly, the rails are what won the war for-"

Bill abruptly turned to leave as he shook his head. "Mr. Walker, I do not mean to be rude, but you speak as though you know the end result of this turmoil, and we both know that's not possible. Am I correct, sir?"

Walker knew he had slipped up . . . again. He had spoken out of 'club time.' He looked around to see if he had been overheard.

Bill leaned closer and said softly, "Walker, for your own good and mine, I'm ending this conversation. I truly enjoy this club. No hassle, no hustle and bustle. It's my few hours each week that I can escape reality. Some people drink to escape, this club is my refuge, and you keep breaking its only rule by speaking out of 'club time.'"

Walker looked embarrassed. "I . . . I try. I just slip up now and then."

"Maybe you're not as at ease as the others, Mr. Walker. You wouldn't be the first person to quit."

"No, no, I really like the club. It's just that I seem to forget and . . . "

Matt approached Walker and said, "Mr. Walker, would you be so kind as to accompany me to the President's office?"

Walker looked lost. "The President's office? Why would he want to see me?"

Walker was escorted away.

Bill shook his head, sank into one of the overstuffed, leather chair and started to read again as thunder rumbled in the background.

A chime sounded and Matt announced, "Dinner is served."

Bill checked his pocket watch and noted to himself, "Eight sharp."

He followed the group into the club's lavish dining room.

The room was just redesigned and all stopped momentarily as they observed the changes for the first time.

The walls were a soft blue wallpaper with embossed white flowers, which ended at a white dental-pattern molding where the wall and ceiling met. The ceiling was white with hand painted doves and blue birds some of which seemed to be perched on the molding while the others flew about.

The long dining table was covered with a Victorian Battenburg Lace tablecloth, which was hand embroidered, as were the lace napkins. In front of each high-backed wooden chair was a place setting, which consisted of Garfield and Humphreys dinner plates and soup bowls decorated with blue flowers, which adorned the plate's edge. In its center was a picture of a group of hounds chasing a fox. The cutlery was vintage Wm Rogers Silverplate silverware. Also next to each setting was a Free-blown, clear Flint Glass ball stem wine glass. A wine decanter, which contained red wine was near the end of the table while another of white wine was at the opposite end.

Over the table hung two brass French nine-candle chandeliers with hanging cut glass decorations.

On each of the four walls hung a large horizontal gold framed Victorian style Rosewood Mirror.

The floor was a dark brown stained bamboo wood with many coats of clear varnish.

Because the night was so wet and damp the fireplace was lit as was the two twelve candelabras on its massive mantle.

The redesign was done by Matt and he watched as the club members were stunned by it. Everything seemed to move as the light from the overhead chandeliers reflected off the mirrors, the white tablecloth, the silverware, dishes and goblets then the highly polished floor. The light from the dancing flames of the fireplace and candelabras joined in to give the room the feeling of movement.

Looking around, Bill saw that Stan Walker was missing. Then he noticed that club president, Prescott Stevens' seat at the head of the table was empty.

As he chose a chair next to Miss Alexander, a thirtyish blonde with an oversized bustle, she turned and said, "Hello, Mr. Scott. Terrible weather, is it not?"

"Certainly is, Miss Alexander."

"Please, call me Jane."

Bill nodded. "And call me Bill," thinking; *Charlene never understood my love of this period. Too bad she couldn't be more like Jane . . . oh well.*

Knowing that Jane's ancestor owned a horse farm in Queens back in 1864 which sold horses to the Union Cavalry he asked, "And tell me, Jane, how goes your horse farm?"

"Quite well, Bill. It's just the cold weather that slows us down. But the Army needs horses and I am fortunate enough to be in the horse selling business." She then turned her attention to Phil Corouso across the table as she said, "Which reminds me, Colonel, could you please enlighten us as to the reason our great President fired General McClellan?"

The colonel furrowed his brow and, sensing that he had just become the center of the table's conversation, pushed back his chair and pronounced, "Well, ma'am, General McClellan was in way over his head, so to speak. He sat still so long that General Lee just built up his resources and struck first. He forced the President's hand."

"Tell me, sir, what would you have done in the general's position?" came a question from Andrew Giddons; an "old money" member whose ancestor's fortune came from the railroads.

The colonel shifted his chair to face Giddons. "I'd have attacked two months ago, sir. The weather was perfect, and he had plenty of manpower and supplies available to him."

Giddons' nod acknowledged his agreement. "And the rails to move them, I might add."

The colonel nodded vigorously, "Absolutely, sir, absolutely. The rails will take the war to a decision on our side, I dare say."

Giddons smiled and raised his glass of wine, saying, "To the railroads of the north!"

The conversation now turned to the dinner selection. The silver edged menu in front of each setting told the club members that tonight's dinner menu is the same as was seen in the St. Nicholas Hotel Dining Room on November 10, 1862.

St. Nicholas Hotel
507-527 Broadway NY, NY
Beverage
White or Red Wine
Soup
Pea Soup, Cabbage Soup
Main Course
Boiled Whitefish, A La Maitre D'Hotel
Or

Boiled Leg of Mutton with Shrimp Sauce

Served With

Small Whole Potatoes, Peas, Corn, Heart of Lettuce With Oil,

Carrots, Brown Gravy

Bread/Rolls

Brown Bread, White Bread, Rolls, Butter

Desert

Orange Icing on Vanilla Ice Cream

Or

Chocklate Cake with Strawberries

Drinks

Tea, Coffee, Milk

Bill was making his selection as the diners heard a new voice say, "I see the war is the topic of the evening, ladies and gentlemen."

Chairs scraped as all turned to see President Prescott Stevens being seated at the head of the table. The guests smiled at him. He signaled a waiter, and dinner was started.

The conversation continued, with the weather and the war being the subjects most discussed. After-dinner cigars were offered along with brandy. Most of the women demurely declined the cigars, the exception being Jane Alexander who easily joined the dozen men at the great, roaring fireplace in the club's den.

President Stevens turned and with an exaggerated bow said, "You grace us with your presence, Miss Alexander."

Jane did a mock curtsy back. "This is the place to be if one wants to learn the inner workings of the world, is it not, President Stevens?"

He smiled at her. "That it is, dear lady, that it is."

Prescott looked quickly around the room and then raised his voice and said somberly, "Mr. Stan Walker left the club this evening. He asked me to say good-bye for him."

No one spoke. The grandfather clock chimed 10 p.m.; watches were taken out of vest pockets, as the guests decided it was getting late. They headed toward the door, but Stevens put a hand on Bill's shoulder.

"Mr. Scott, will you stay behind? I'd have a word with you, if possible."

Bill looked questioning but said, "Certainly, President Stevens." He mentally shrugged his shoulders and thought, *it's not like I have a warm reception waiting for me back at the apartment.*

They turned back into the den. Prescott pulled a thick velvet sash on the wall, and Matt appeared.

"Sir, you rang?"

"Yes, Matt, another brandy for me and whatever Mr. Scott prefers."

"Brandy is fine," Bill replied.

As Matt closed the door behind him, Stevens walked toward two wingback chairs in front of the fire and settled into one. "I've had a long day and shall have my nightcap seated," he said. He indicated the other chair to Bill and added, "Sit, sir. Relax."

Bill sat in the warm chair. Matt returned, served the brandies, and Stevens raised his toward Bill and said, "Cheers."

"Cheers," Bill responded.

Prescott took a sip and said thoughtfully, "Two years tonight."

"Excuse me?"

"Two years tonight. It's your anniversary, sir. Two years ago this evening you joined the club."

Bill smiled. "Yes, two years tonight. I was wondering why you asked me to stay behind. Is this the norm for someone's anniversary?"

"No, sir, it is not. May I address you by your given name? William, is it not?"

"My friends call me Bill, but if you prefer William, that's fine."

"Bill it is and I'm Prescott, at least when we are alone. I must keep to being the head of the club in front of the members, and perceived familiarity breeds relaxation of the club's rules. Would you agree?"

Bill nodded. "Oh I do agree, Prescott. May I ask why Mr. Walker left the club?"

"Yes, you may. In fact, I took his key. He was asked to leave. He could not keep the rule. He kept speaking out of 'club time.' But you knew that didn't you?"

Bill looked at him nervously. "Yes, I knew that. Do you think I spoke out of 'club time' with him tonight? Because if you do . . ."

"No, not at all, Bill. In fact, I believe that you have never slipped up."

"Then why did you ask me to stay? Surely not just to ask me to renew my membership?"

Prescott took a deep pull of his drink and put it down. He leaned toward Bill. "No, not to renew. I have no problem filling the club's memberships. There's a very long waiting list of potential members. In fact, I'd like to ask you to play a little game with me."

Bill was puzzled. "What kind of a game?"

"Well, pretty much the same kind of game you play every time you enter the club. The game of make-believe."

Bill raised his eyebrows. "Make-believe?"

Prescott rested his on his elbows on knees, chin resting on his clasped hands. "Yes, Bill, make-believe. Every time you come here you pretend you are back in the 1800s. A time of quiet streets, no blaring radio, cell phones, TV, car horns, a make-believe time trip back to gentler times. Am I right?"

Now Bill leaned forward. "Then yes, I do play a make-believe game. I guess we all do."

"Some of us better than others. Some of us are so good at this, that if they suddenly found themselves back in 1862, they could carry on as though they belonged there."

"I guess you're right."

Then with a sense of purpose, Prescott rose and said, "Bill, please follow me to my office."

They went up the heavily carpeted staircase that was off-limits to club members. An ornate key attached to Prescott by a thick gold chain around his neck opened a heavy mahogany door with highly shined brass doorknobs and hinges. Gas lamps lit the room. All the furniture, except for the television, was from the 1800s. The tall windows had floor-to-ceiling dark brown drapes and the walls were covered with tan and brown wallpaper with flocked trees and wood scenes. Paintings that depicted horses pulling carriages along country roads and streets hung on the high walls and the floor was covered in typical Victorian style wall-to-wall brown rug. But it was the furniture that amazed Bill and he whistled in admiration.

"Federal pieces! Where did you ever get them? They are priceless! I know. I have a coat tree, and it set me back some. These look brand new."

Prescott smiled. "Would you like this desk?" he said as he patted the top.

"It's yours, Bill. No charge. I can get another anytime I want."

Bill looked confused. He knew the market fairly well and was certain there was no way there could be two desks like this one.

"If I'm correct that desk is an A.H. Andrews Roll Top desk. I've only seen pictures of them as they are extremely rare."

"You are correct, sir." Prescott went around to a chair behind his desk and motioned for Bill to sit in another of the period pieces.

"Please, Bill, sit. And I mean it. This desk is yours. No charge. You see I watch each and every member of the club. I watch to see how well they stay in character and you are simply the best! In all the time the club has been around, I've never seen a person adapt so well. When you are here, you are truly in the 1800s. As I said you are simply, the best."

"So I win the antique desk because I'm good at keeping the rule?"

"First of all, it's not an antique, it's modern."

"You mean it's a knockoff? A copy made in China or somewhere?"

"No, I mean it's a modern piece for the 1800s."

"But this is the 21st century . . . not the 19th century."

"Where? You mean here? In this club? But you say you believe this is the 1800s every time you come here."

"Yes, but, I mean, it's really 2011, not 1862."

Prescott pointed to the door they had come in. "Out there, the way we came in, that's 2011." He turned and pointed to another door on the far wall. "Out that door is the year 1862."

Bill looked at the far door, then back at Prescott. "Out that door is 1862?"

Prescott nodded. "Yes. And that's where I can get another desk, another wingback chair or clothes tree. Right out there."

Bill laughed. "Well, Prescott . . . you got me. I love the club, I really do. And I kind of had you on a pedestal before this evening. But now . . . well, I really don't know what to do. I wish we could have kept this on the level it was before tonight. It was more enjoyable just coming here and playing dress up." He got up to leave.

"So, now you're quitting?" Prescott said with raised eyebrows. "Taking the easy way out? I can't believe I was wrong. I had you as the adventurous type. An ex-U.S. Navy SEAL turned reporter whose hobby is the 1800s. Liked it so much he would jump at the chance to live in that time period. Am I wrong?"

"No, you are right," Bill answered. "But I don't believe what you are proposing is true. I think this is some kind of a test . . . a test to see if I'll talk out of 'club time,' right?"

"Couldn't be more mistaken, sir. What I'm proposing is true. And I believe you're interested in hearing me out." He looked intently at Bill. "I've studied you, and I pride myself on my accurate assessments of people. What I'm telling you is something that the average person just could not comprehend."

Bill sat back down. The room's curtains were open and he looked out the window at the rain. "Well, the weather tells me to stay at least until it lets up. So I might as well hear you out."

Prescott seemed relieved and sat back. "Good, Bill, good. Now, I'd like to tell you a story. I come from 1863. I was like you in a sense . . . a happy bachelor with a good job. I was a history teacher in New York. One day a man introduced himself to me in a restaurant I frequented. His name was John Smith, so he said, and he also was a history teacher. He told me he was the father of one of my past students, Harold Smith, who was killed in the war, but always spoke highly of me." He paused a moment then continued as he sat forward. "I felt that he was a sick man for he constantly fought for air as he spoke." He sat back as he went on. "He visited me for short visits over the next few weeks, and after gaining my confidence, he told me a different story . . . an entirely different story, believe me! I was, as you are, shocked to hear it. But I did, as you did, sit back and listen. He said that his real name was James Prescott. He said he was a future Prescott, a future relative of mine. He claimed to live in the year 2060! I thought it was preposterous and told him so. He said he understood my stance, of course, but was willing to prove it to me. Would I accompany him to his home? As I said, he had gained my confidence and, as it was a short carriage ride, I accompanied him to his home." He grinned as he patted the desk once again. "This very building."

The grandfather clock chimed eleven times and the storm outside was still in full force.

Prescott does tell a good yarn, Bill thought. *He's probably a lonely guy with good taste in furniture and bad taste in sci-fi stories, hoping I can get it published for him.*

Prescott continued, "James Prescott, of the future, showed me a door in his den and said it opened to the future. I, of course, was a non-believer, as are you, until he opened the door. He took me down a flight of stairs and opened a second door that led to a garden surrounded by a high stonewall fence outside of which was a well-lighted street. No cobblestone street was this, nor was it asphalt as you are used to. Rather, it was a light blue, plastic-like substance, which glowed, giving off enough illumination that no gaslights were needed. The first thing I noticed was the smell, or rather the lack of smell. No horse manure! I never realized how one became so used to the stench. Why, in my time it was just there! Always there! And now, well it was truly a breath of fresh air. But here was the bad part. The people of the future had cleaned up their atmosphere so well that there was no pollution. Why the air was so clean that I had a hard time breathing it. It was as though I were on top of Mount Everest. Of course I was never on the mountain, but they assured me that the air they breathed was so clean that I couldn't stay there long nor could they stay in my time for too long a spell. An automobile glided soundlessly by, borne not on wheels nor powered by a pollution producing engine, but on shafts of compressed air. People were walking casually around, not in a so-called 'New York Minute,' but leisurely. They wore close fitting, one-piece suits with shoes. It was fantastic to say the very least! I was overwhelmed, and seeing this, he smiled and escorted me back inside where my breathing was much improved. He assured me that I was now back in the 1800s, and proved it by opening the front door through which we had entered. It was a dark night of 1863 lighted only by gas lamps with horse-drawn carriages rumbling by on cobblestones and the familiar smells of my time. He gave me a brandy, and we sat by his fireplace as he explained all."

Prescott took a sip of his drink, and Bill reached for his. *Not a bad story,* he thought. *Wonder where it's going?*

The club's president rested his drink on the desk. "It seems that overall; the 1800s were in many ways a key to the future . . . the future as we know it now. He told me that this time period saw many inventions that would shape the world all the way up to 2060 and beyond. He showed me points in history that were crucial to the development of the human race.

Bill interrupted him. "Tell me a few."

Prescott started ticking off on his fingers, "Cotton gin, use of peanuts, steel-hulled ships, development of steam power, development of the railroads, ending slavery . . ."

"Okay, okay, I get it," Bill said.

"As I was saying," Prescott went on, "it was a period that was extremely important to the world. And at times it needed help."

"Help? Help from whom?"

"Help from the people of 2060, that's who. There were times when history needed a hand because it veered off course."

"But if it was helped when it was veering off course, wasn't that sort of changing history? And if you were changing . . . oh boy, you got me. I'm starting to react as though your story is for real." Bill looked at his watch. "I really have to go. It's getting late and I have a deadline tomorrow."

Prescott shook his head. "Tomorrow may never come. I believe you are as ready as I was to take a glimpse back." He gestured toward the door as he stood up. "Shall we?"

Bill smiled and, with some reluctance, followed him to the large mahogany door on the far side of the den. Prescott took out the gold chain, and Bill saw that there was a second key was on it. Prescott turned that key in the lock and opened the door a crack.

"Ready, Bill?"

"Sure, but I hope you don't have any skeletons in your closet," he joked.

The door was opened wider, revealing a flight of descending stairs.

"Allow me to go first, Bill?" Prescott asked.

"Please do, Prescott," Bill replied.

They went down the stone steps flanked on either side by a red brick wall that was illuminated by hissing brass and decorated-glass gas lamps. The stairs ended in front of a large steel security door. Prescott unlocked this door with the same key but before opening it, he turned to Bill and asked, "Set, sir? Set to walk the streets of 1863?"

DATELINE: NOVEMBER 10, 1863 10:00 A.M. PLACE: THE 1800 CLUB'S GARDEN, NEW YORK CITY

Bill nodded, and Prescott pushed the door open onto a high-walled sleeping garden. The path of small flat stones showed Bill where the various flowers would grow in the summer and there were tall evergreens planted along the inside of the garden's high wall. Bill spotted a few Black-capped Chickadee and Northern Cardinals flitting from tree to tree.

A small pond was in the corner and he spotted two goldfish hibernating beneath the frozen water.

As they stepped out of the shaded area Bill held his hand up to cover his eyes from the morning sun. He could hear a horse-drawn carriage clattering by on cobblestones. He slowly followed Prescott toward a high wrought iron gate. Prescott opened the gate with the same key, and then flung his arms wide and proclaimed, "Voila! Welcome to 1863, Mr. Bill Scott."

They stepped out onto the sidewalk, which was composed of large, flat, gray slabs of slate. Bill looked around in disbelief.

"But, but how can the sun be up? It's after eleven at night!" He shook his head as he looked around. "It's true! My God, man, it's true! You did it . . . I can't believe it." The flowers feebly masked the smell that finally reached Bill.

"Horse manure! My God, it stinks!" He looked around and tried to breathe through his mouth as his eyes filled with tears. Prescott offered him a handkerchief.

"It takes time, Bill. Breathe slowly."

Bill wiped his eyes and did as Prescott said; took slow deliberate breaths. *It's mind over matter,* he thought.

He saw two women walking slowly towards them, arm in arm. Prescott gave a hint of a bow. Both were about ten years younger than Bills' thirty-two years.

"Good day, Miss Davenport, Miss Jenkins. Nice day for a walk, is it not?"

Both answered, "Good day, Mr. Stevens."

Miss Davenport added, "Yes, it's a beautiful day for a walk."

Prescott turned to Bill. "A colleague of mine, Mr. Scott. He just arrived from a long trip. A very long trip."

The young lady smiled at Bill. "Did you come by boat, Mr. Scott?"

"Uh . . . no, I took the train and a carriage," Bill answered, trying to collect himself. "Best way to travel these days, I would say."

The women nodded in unison and began to wander off. "Good day, gentlemen," they said, with Miss Jenkins adding, "Enjoy our fair town, Mr. Scott."

"I will, ma'am, I will," Bill replied. He was still wide-eyed as he watched them cross the street. They picked up their long skirts a tiny bit and stepped gingerly over and around the horse manure, which literally covered the street. The clop of hooves got his attention and he saw a horse-drawn, creaking flatbed wagon coming along the street. It carried a load of furniture and he spotted the white hand written lettering on the side, which read: SMITH'S MOVING CO. The driver had a long red mustache and beard and he tried his best to go around the horse waste and missing cobblestones.

As the wagon went by Bill spotted two boys and a girl hanging from the rear of the wagon. One boy put his finger to his lips as though telling Bill to keep quiet lest the driver discover the added weight. Coming in the opposite direction was a small black two-wheel carriage pulled by a white horse with a bobbed tail. The driver was a young man wearing a long black overcoat with a black wool collar and cuffs. His tall black hat sat firmly on his well-trimmed brown hair. He also sported a mustache.

Sitting next to him was a young lady dressed in a white outfit with a fur collar and muff to keep her hands warm. On her head was a high white hat with a single red feather in it. It was hard to see her face as she wore a thick white scarf around her neck that also covered her mouth and nose. Unlike the horse that pulled the moving company's wagon this horse pranced along as it pulled the fairly light carriage.

Bill turned to Prescott and said, "How . . . I mean . . . well, I guess I do mean, how . . . how did it happen? How did we go from 2011 to 1863 just by walking out a door?"

"Not just a door, Bill. A time-changing portal! Let's go back upstairs while I explain as much as I can to you."

He closed and locked the gate.

Bill was still awed by the sights . . . and the smell. "This is utterly fantastic!" he exclaimed as he once again wiped his eyes and followed Prescott back into the garden. Bill noted that Prescott fiddled with a small object as they walked towards the door.

DATELINE: NOVEMBER 10, 2011 11:37 P.M. PLACE: THE 1800 CLUB, NEW YORK CITY

They sat in the club's den. Coffee had been served, and they were once again in front of the roaring fireplace.

Bill was still incredulous as he wiped his watery eyes. "Please explain, Prescott. This is beyond my wildest dreams. Has anyone else from the club gone back?"

"Just a few: three men and one woman.

"Are they still in the club?"

"No, unfortunately one was killed in an auto accident, the woman left New York when her husband's job was moved, and the others just got too elderly for the trips."

Prescott sat back and looked at the fire. "The club is a place that has been set up to be able to find people who have no problem traveling to and from the past. It is a continuous job interview so to speak."

Scott asked, "So, did I pass the interview?"

"With flying colors," came the answer.

Bill pressed him, saying, "I really need more information about this. I mean, is the government behind this?"

"No! And they must never know of it," Stevens said with alarm. "I've been directed to keep this just between any chosen traveler and myself. My Lord, why, if the government knew of this, we'd have troops stationed in ancient Rome!"

Bill laughed. "I'm ex-Navy SEAL so I know where you're coming from. They mean well, but it just seems to go bad when they meddle in things. So who's the big honcho? There has to be a top guy. Right?"

"Well, not so much a top guy as a top group. Tell me, Bill, do you believe in alternate worlds?"

"You mean another world just like ours but where history took a different course? Heck, yesterday I would have said no, but today I think anything is possible."

Prescott smiled. "Well, not only is it possible, but I've seen it. And that's the mission of the club. You see, when the group first invented the time exchanger and started sending probes back, they saw that at times a few of the key historic people didn't do what our history books said they did. So they realized that someone was either writing the history books wrong, or someone was going back and helping those key historic people do as they were supposed to do. The group concluded that the history books were not wrong, so the people somehow were being persuaded to do as our history books said they did. Therefore, a time traveler who knew of our present history books, helped out. Understand?"

"Yes, sort of . . . but what if the 'helping hand' person got sick or something, and he didn't get the chance to do the 'helping hand' thing, what then?"

"Oh, it has happened. And then they have to send someone else. The problem is that if historical people are interfered with too many times, they get suspicious of strangers and that causes other troubles. It tends to change them."

"How so?" Bill queried.

"Well, perhaps they are an adventurous type with a devil-may-care attitude. If they are interfered with, they may become suspicious of others and alter history by shying away from crowds. What if George Washington had become suspicious of his troops? Would he have been able to lead them if he had shunned them? Would he have been able to persuade them to stay at Valley Forge for that long, cold winter? See what I mean? That's why we are so meticulous about the people we choose to take a trip."

"Trip? You mean like we just did?"

"More, much more. I'm talking about mingling with the people from the 1800s. You know, Bill, to you they were just people long gone. Just written pieces of history. But you go through that door and you are with living, breathing everyday people. They eat and drink, have likes and dislikes just as we do. That's the real purpose of this club. To find the person who fits easily into another time, without anyone from that selected period ever suspecting a thing. Do you feel you can do that, Bill?"

"Heck, yes! What do I have to do?"

Prescott offered him a cigar and then lit it. He sat back and puffed it to life and as he looked at Bill through a ring of smoke, said, "What do you have to do? Simple. You have to give the Gettysburg Address. Do you know it?"

Bill looked back, stunned. "Do I know the Gettysburg Address? No. Who really can recite the entire address? No one I know."

Prescott pointed to the bookcases that lined the walls. "It's all in there," he said.

"Wait a second," Bill said. "What do you mean *give* the Gettysburg Address? Are you or the group trying to . . . to . . . change history?"

Prescott tapped some ash from his cigar as he shook his head. "No, we want to get history back on course. You see, history tells us that Lincoln was a very depressed man. What wasn't known was that when he was in his depressed state, he would sleep for hours at a time even during the day, and forget many things he did when he was awake. He just could not function. There were times when his bouts of depression had him down for weeks at a time."

Prescott flicked some ash off his jacket and continued, "Well, one of our probes showed that he never made the Gettysburg Address. It seems that when he was supposed to give the famous speech, he was in the grip of depression. He never got to give it, and that was just one of many reasons that the British felt they could enter the war on the side of the South, and the North had to settle for a stalemate. The United States of 2066 would be a split union. Not still at war, of course, but with different trading partners, politics, money system and many other things. The U.S. of the North would not have been the superpower we see today. This and many other things have made the group decide to send someone back to take Abraham Lincoln's place and make the famous speech."

Bill asked in a low voice, "And you think I'm that guy?"

"Yes, we do."

"You're crazy," Bill said emphatically. "I'd never pull it off. Why his Secret Service guys . . . "

"First, there wasn't any Secret Service at that time. The U.S. Army protected him. However, he did have a private detective of sorts that looked after him, and he's in on it."

Bill was stunned once again. "He's in on it? What do you mean?"

"We simply had to tell him. I can take you back, but you still have to get into the White House and switch places with the President of the Union. We had to tell him."

"Tell him what? That I'm going to take the President's place?"

Prescott nodded. "Yes, of course. They know how he gets. It's their job to keep it a secret. It's their sworn duty to protect the President and the Union. Knowing that the country is being run by a person who suffers from depression, they are protecting him from being looked upon as a weakling by the world."

"So you told the top security guy?"

"Yes, in fact, I dined with the head of White House security last night." He held a hand up as he corrected himself, "Well, actually last night, one hundred and forty years ago."

Bill took a drink of his brandy. "This is too much," he said.

"You can handle it, Bill. I have faith in you."

"I still can't believe this." He sat forward. "What did the security guy say when you said you were from the future? I mean did he freak out?"

"Why? Why would he, 'freak out,' as you say? The only thing different between him and you is the one hundred plus years. He's a smart man, and after I took him through the door to this period, he was in all the way. So, to answer your question, no, he didn't freak out. He was happy to know that his generation was being watched and helped from a future time."

"So, *1984* hadn't been written yet."

Prescott grinned. "No, he doesn't know of 'Big Brother' yet. But I feel that he'd be all for it." He stretched out his legs, as the clock struck again. "When I told him of your pending visit, he said he'd take care of the switch."

"I guess you were pretty sure I'd be the guy to do it. Even before you told me."

"As I said, Bill, your temperament showed me you were the right person for this job."

"But I don't even look like Lincoln."

"That's easy. You are pretty close to his height and from a distance with a little touching up you'll do fine."

"Does his wife know?"

"No, she's going to be out of Washington that day, and Lincoln was to leave for Gettysburg early in the morning before the city really got moving. It'll be you and the security men."

"But, his voice! I don't have a clue what he sounds like. Do you?"

"No, but that day, Lincoln, that is you, will have a cold that will keep him covering his mouth with a handkerchief."

Bill was becoming more interested. "Well let's say I'm in, what's the plan?"

Prescott continued, "We will meet with Kenneth Reilly, his security man, and he'll brief you as to your mannerisms . . . that is, Lincoln's mannerisms. He will give us the plan for the switch and we'll go from there."

"If I do this, I have a request," Bill said. "I want to spend some time there. I mean, back there."

Prescott shook his head vigorously, "No! Too dangerous. You have to operate out of the club and return as soon as possible. Besides, the group in the future would be dead against it."

"Then I won't do it."

Prescott raised one eyebrow. "You won't do it? Are you telling me you don't want to walk the streets of 1863 to see what it's really like? I believe you should rethink it, Bill. This is a once-in-a-lifetime trip. Pass it up and you will live the rest of your life regretting it."

Bill looked at the door and, after a pause, said, "You're right. But if I didn't insist, I'd spend the rest of my life regretting it."

As both men looked at each other, Prescott grinned. "A modern day Mexican standoff, so to speak."

Bill finished his drink and put down the glass, signaling his determination. "Prescott, if I'm as good as you think I am, you'll get me some time back there. You know I won't mess up."

"Damn, man. You must understand the gravity of the situation. One slip, one ounce of suspicion from any of the locals and . . . and . . . why, we just don't know what will happen."

"Know what, Prescott? You said you're from the 1800s. Am I right?"

Prescott nodded reluctantly. "Yes, yes, I am. But what's that have to do with . . . "

Bill continued to present his argument. "With me going back for a bit, on my own? Well, you did it. You came forward and didn't mess up. What makes you think I'll blow it?"

"Because I had the club to retreat to if I felt out of place. When the fast moving automobiles, high-flying aircraft and loud motorcycles put me in a panic, I simply retreated into the club and settled down. Should you travel on your own and get a sort of panic attack, why, what would you do?"

"I think there's a big difference, Prescott, between what you did and what I'm proposing to do. I've had the time to study the past while you had no way to prepare for the future. It seems to me that you had a much tougher time of it than I would. Don't you agree?"

Prescott shrugged. "Yes, I agree you would be more prepared than I was. But they have rules."

"Then why doesn't one of them go back and fix it?"

Prescott finished his drink and shook his head. "They can't. You see, as I said, after years of polluting the air and oceans, mankind smartened up and passed stringent laws against polluting, and enforced them. The laws worked so well that the air that people from your future era breathe is cleaner than it's been in hundreds of years. Because people from their group were raised in such a clean atmosphere, when they traveled back to my time, or earlier, they felt they were suffocating. So they could bear it for only a short time, not long enough for a mission. To keep history on track, they sent back mechanical probes to check historical facts. When they saw a problem developing, they knew they had to send back someone to help straighten it out. That was another problem. Since none of them could stay back in time long enough to fix it, they decided to seek help from someone of that period. I was selected to be that person. I did some 'saves' over the years; but over time, I realized I needed help. People who had various aptitudes were needed to make the missions a success. So I sold the Time Watchers on backing a club for recruits."

"Without the club members knowing it." Bill added.

"Yes, of course. I mean, I couldn't really advertise that I was looking for time travelers, could I? Would you have joined the 1800 Club reading that advertisement?"

Bill shook his head and said, "No, guess not."

"That's why I set up the club."

"To start your own farm team."

"Farm team? I don't follow you."

Bill explained, "Baseball talk for training up-and-coming possibilities for their team."

"Oh, I see. Well then, yes. The group did set up this club to attract certain types of people. People who could operate in the time that needed attention. People who could blend in and complete the mission."

"And you are the person who selects that person. Correct?"

"Correct. I am that person. And, correct again, sir, I believe that you could travel around in that period and be accepted as one of them. Therefore Bill, I shall allow you to do just that. But after I buy you lunch at my favorite restaurant in 1863. Agree?"

Bill smiled broadly. "Agree!"

The clock struck once again and Prescott shook his head and laughed. "However, not this evening. It's way past my bedtime. Tomorrow, say, 11 am?"

"You're on! Where?"

"Come to the club and change. Matt will bring you to me and I suggest you wear walking shoes. Till then, Bill, pleasant dreams."

The two men shook hands and Bill left the club, tired yet completely awake.

For Bill, the next morning took a long time to arrive. Finally, dressed in the clothes of a gentleman of the mid-1800s, he stood with Matt as he knocked on the big wooden door. Prescott opened it and said, "Good morning, Bill." He gestured him into the room as Matt left and closed the door behind him. They shook hands.

"Good morning, Prescott."

"Are you ready for a leisurely lunch?"

"I ate hardly anything all morning," Bill said. "I still can't believe it."

Prescott unlocked the door at the rear of his den and went through, as Bill followed close behind. At the bottom of the stairs Bill once again saw him fidget with a small pocket watch of sorts before opening the solid security door.

DATELINE: July 30, 1863, 11:00 A.M. PLACE: The 1800 CLUB'S GARDEN, NEW YORK CITY

They entered the sun filled garden and went out through the iron-gated entrance in the wall. Prescott locked it behind them and tucked the key inside his starched shirt. He smiled at Bill and said, "Shall we dine, sir?"

"A wonderful idea, Prescott. Which place do you prefer?"

"The Botterhouse Restaurant over on Worth Street," came the answer. "Bit of a walk but worth the trip. Up to it?"

"Lead on, Prescott, lead on."

They walked downtown and Bill was agog at seeing sights he had only dreamed of or had seen only in black-and-white, grainy photos. That's when it hit him; everything was in color! Living color! He was used to looking at black and white photographs of the era and here it was in every day color! He was surprised at the variety of colors they wore. Bright yellows and reds replaced the flat dark colors that appeared in the old photos.

Prescott was right. The people were real, as real as anyone Bill had ever encountered. But the air was even more horrible than he thought it would be. Horse waste was giving off a scent that individuals were fighting with overpowering perfumed scents of their own. *It's a battle they're losing,* Bill thought as he covered his nose with his handkerchief as though he had a cold. Birds sat on trees overhanging the streets and added to the waste.

The noise of the city was also different. No automobiles or bus engine noise, no horns or underground train noises. He could hear horses braying and the clopping of their hooves on cobblestones.

But this noise was all on a smaller scale than he was used to hearing. He found he could hear the people as they chatted amongst themselves without having to shout over the noise of a busy street of his time.

Still, Bill was part of it. He was one of them. People walked past him with parcels under their arms. He was happily surprised to note that they were not staring at him. He truly was one of them . . . and he loved it! He noticed that they all did the same thing when crossing the street - look left and right then down to step around and over the horse waste or missing cobble stones. The horse waste was everywhere, as were the thousands of flies it brought. Still, he loved every minute of it!

All the while, Prescott was giving a running commentary as they worked their way toward the restaurant. They turned right on Worth Street, leaving Broadway behind. The old buildings that Bill remembered were now new. Many had long, high sets of stone steps and banisters going up to second floor doors. *Too bad they would be torn down,* he thought, *to make way for the wider streets of the future.* He took note that even though the weather was warm, the city was powered by coal burning furnaces and the soot they gave off was horrendous. The black smoke, which belched from the chimneys, darkened the buildings' facades and tended to mix with the already foul air.

Prescott started to cross the street, but stepped quickly out of the way of a horse team pulling a wagon loaded with kegs of beer. When it had passed, he and Bill headed across to the open door of the Botterhouse Restaurant. The sidewalk menu boasted the freshest leg of mutton in New York City. On entering, a rotund man in a red vest greeted them.

"Good day, Mr. Stevens. Have you been out of town? Haven't seen too much of you lately."

"Yes, Timmy, I've been visiting my sister over in New Jersey. How's business?"

"Couldn't be better, sir. Just got some of your favorite liver in yesterday. Got it before Linden's Restaurant even knew it was available. Interested?"

Prescott patted his ample stomach. "Now, that sounds like a great lunch. My friend and I would like to sit by the window, if possible. He's from New Jersey and doesn't get to see much of our town."

Timmy ushered them around full tables to a window seat facing Worth Street. The windows all had their red and white striped awnings down, trying, in vain, to keep the sun's heat out of the restaurant. He gave them menus and then went to attend to other customers.

Bill focused on the specials written on the chalkboard and said, "Leg of lamb, roasted potatoes, cabbage and carrots smothered in a thick brown gravy. Chicken soup and a special Botterhouse greens dish with their own secret dressing . . . no burger and fries, I take it?"

Prescott smiled. "Not yet. But, the liver and onions is done with true love here, and I haven't had any in over three weeks. It's also not as heavy as the lamb dish."

"Sounds good. I'll have that, too," Bill said.

"And a beer?"

"Sure, that'd be perfect."

After the meal, Prescott sat back and offered Bill a cigar. "No law against smoking in restaurants yet, Bill. Have one?"

"Don't mind if I do."

They both lit up, as Timmy reappeared.

"So, gentlemen, how was your lunch? Satisfactory, I hope."

Prescott once again patted his stomach, "My Lord, Tim, you have outdone yourself. I don't think I'll be having anything to eat for . . . for . . . well, at least until this evening."

Timmy and Bill laughed at the man making fun of himself. Prescott paid the cashier and left a tip for Timmy who quickly pocketed it as they went out into the bright sunny day.

"Prescott, that was magnificent! Can we stroll for a bit?"

"A bit is about all I can do, Bill. I have a game knee that keeps me sitting a lot."

Their attention was taken by the sound of a marching band. Coming up the street toward them was a military band followed by a group of men in civilian clothes being marched by a grizzled old sergeant as best he could. Running alongside the column were excited children.

Prescott frowned as they passed. "Poor sods," he said. "Marching blithely off to victory and glory. Of course, getting maimed or killed is not on the recruiting posters. And to think that more Americans will be killed in this war than in any other future war."

Bill looked at him. "Talking out of 'club time,' Prescott. That could get you kicked out, you know."

Prescott laughed and slapped Bill's back. "Ha! Right you are my friend, right you are. Must remember where, or rather, what period I'm in." Then, becoming serious, he said, "It's just the knowledge of knowing there's nothing we can do to undo the bad parts that we know are coming." He shook his head. "Frustrating!"

Bill nodded in agreement.

A rumble of thunder threatened their walk, and Bill reluctantly offered to end it prematurely. Prescott agreed and they turned back.

Once back in the garden Bill saw Prescott take out the small watch-like item from his inside jacket pocket and after pressing some buttons opened the security door and they entered the stairway.

DATELINE: NOVEMBER 11, 2011, 2:30 P.M. PLACE: THE 1800 CLUB, NEW YORK CITY

Back in the club sipping a brandy, Bill stared into his drink and said, "Amazing. Breakfast in 2011, lunch and a stroll in 1863 and brandy back in 2011. Amazing."

Smiling, Prescott queried, "Are you ready to take the trip, Bill?"

"Absolutely! When?"

"November nineteenth."

"Two weeks away.

"No, I mean November nineteenth their time. You can go whenever you are ready. I can avail you of our very extensive library. It also contains the complete speech by Lincoln at Gettysburg."

"I do need to go over that. What do you do to get me to the time needed? Sort of dial it up?" Bill asked.

Prescott explained, "A good analogy. I have a TFM, short for Time Frequency Modulator. With it, I can dial up any time I wish, back until 1820. That's when this building was built. We can go back earlier, but as there are no buildings around before that time we will step out into a clearing surrounded by a small group of trees. The TFM has been entrusted to me by the Time Watchers of the future."

"I would love to take a look at it," Bill said.

Prescott looked at him pensively. "You will, and I hope that soon it will be yours."

"Mine?" Bill wasn't sure he had heard correctly.

"Yes. You see, as I said, this is an interview. The job consists of not only doing what's asked of you in the past from time to time, but also running this club."

"Running this club? What do you mean?"

"Simple, Bill. I'm tired. I want to spend more time with my family . . . back in 1860. I've had a great experience over the past twenty-five of your years. I've traveled extensively and met some of the most important people in history. But I'm tired. And part of my job was to watch for someone to inherit the club. And Bill, I think you are that person, as do the History Watchers."

"They know about me?"

"Yes, of course. We had a meeting yesterday, and they went over your records. With my recommendation they agreed that you would be the best person to run the club. What do you say?"

"I . . . I don't know. What do I have to do? I mean, my job, my apartment . . . "

"This will be your job. At whatever your price, although money for living expenses will not be needed. The club has been owned privately since the very beginning. The dues more than cover the costs. And as for your apartment, this is a six story Townhouse in the heart of New York City. And all you have to do is, when contacted by the future people about a kink in time, fix it. Any more questions?"

"Just a million or so," Bill said. "But if I accept, what happens to you?"

"I'll be going back to my time." He sighed as he spread his hands wide. "Bill, this is a wonderful period that you are from, but I do miss the slower pace of the 1800s. I'm sure you understand."

Bill raised his eyebrows and asked, "Are you financially all right?"

Prescott laughed heartily. "I'm fine. I have all I'll ever need. I'm supposed to live another twenty plus years, and I want to be with my sister and her family at Port Monmouth, New Jersey enjoying the shore."

Bill's mouth dropped. "You . . . you know when . . . when . . . "

"When I'm going to die? Yes, July 9, 1886. In Port Monmouth, New Jersey, while at the beach. The papers will say I passed quietly while napping on a blanket on the beach with my sister and her grandchildren. I had to look it up. Just had to."

Bill nodded. "Yes, I guess I would have to, too. I'm sorry."

Waving off Bill's concern, Prescott said, "Sorry for what? Sorry that I died? I did, in your history, but as you can see I'm still very much a warm-blooded being just like you. Now, let's get down to business. First put these on." Prescott passed him a long coat and tall hat from the 1860s as he explained, "I had Matt provide us both with long coats and hats as we will be going back to November and it gets quite chilly."

They both buttoned up the long coats and put on their hats.

"Ready?"

"Ready!" Bill answered.

Prescott took a small pocket watch-sized unit out of his pocket and showed it to Bill. On the face were number pads.

"The Time Frequency Modulator, or TFM. Now, to open the portal, you simply type in the date and time you want then depress the 'Activate' button. As I said, this building was built in 1820, and the door is always the way into and out of the period you selected."

"Does the TFM have to be recharged?"

"No never. But the next thing you have to do is memorize Lincoln's speech." Prescott handed Bill a small notebook. "I've picked up a copy from our archives. When you are ready, we'll schedule the trip. Meanwhile, we have a meeting with the security gentleman in one hour."

Bill flipped through the pages. "I'm a quick study. I'll have it memorized by tomorrow morning. I can't wait to meet him."

Prescott led him back to the door. "One more thing Bill, your resume states that you are single. Is that still correct?"

Bill nodded his head and smiled, "Yes, that's correct. And it'll be this way for a long time."

Bill followed Prescott to the door in the den and they went down the stone stairs. Once at the bottom landing Prescott handed him the TFM.

"Here, type in November 2, 11:00 A.M. and press the 'Activate' button."

Bill followed his instructions and after depressing the 'Activate' button, opened the security door.

DATELINE: NOVEMBER 2, 1863 11:00 A.M. PLACE: THE 1800 CLUB'S GARDEN, NEW YORK CITY

It was a sunny but chilly day in 1863 and the garden was sleeping. The two time travelers walked to the gate.

"Shall we walk over to Central Park, Bill?"

"It is a beautiful day and I'd love to take in the sights, Prescott."

The walk was slower than it should have been but Prescott grinned to himself as he knew a new time traveler would try to see everything at once. They finally entered the park and Prescott stopped at an empty bench.

"Shall we sit a bit?"

A little boy ran by, frightening a flock of birds into the air as his nanny chased after him. The birds fluttered over the large park bench and Bill and Prescott ducked instinctively. A man dressed in a brown, three-piece suit with matching cravat over his heavily starched white shirt strolled by and nodded at a woman pushing a baby carriage. He stopped and smiled at Prescott as he tipped his top hat. "Good day, sir. Are you waiting for someone or may I sit a spell?"

Prescott tipped his hat in response. "Please, I insist. It's a beautiful day and one simply could not enjoy New York better than by sitting in the park." He turned to Bill and asked, "Don't you agree, Bill?"

"I do, I do. One should live each day as though it's the first day of the rest of his life."

The man looked at him admiringly. "Well said, sir. Well said." He reached into his breast pocket and took out a small, silver calling-card case and flipped it open in his palm.

"Kenneth Reilly. My card, gentlemen."

Both men accepted a card, and Prescott turned to the man with a similar case, saying, "And mine, sir."

The two men shook hands as Bill patted his breast pocket. "Blast! I seem to have left mine in my other jacket." He read the card in his hand, as he introduced himself. "I am Bill Scott. I write for a small newspaper based in Chicago, Mr. Reilly. Pleased to make your acquaintance."

"The pleasure is mine, sir." The two shook hands.

Prescott smiled at Reilly. "All is well, Mr. Reilly?" he asked.

The newcomer nodded, "As well as can be, sir." He tipped his head towards Bill and said, "This, then is the person who will step in for my employer?"

"He is."

Reilly looked at Bill, and Bill returned the gaze. Reilly was stocky with jet-black hair streaked with white through his beard and mustache. His handshake was powerful, and Bill felt that Reilly was sending him a message. Bill's handshake was as firm as the security man's and Reilly nodded in acknowledgment.

"A powerful grip for a newspaperman," he said.

"From setting lead type on deadlines," Bill responded.

Reilly addressed Bill in a low voice. "Prescott has told me a mighty wild tale, sir. I thought him to be one of the new science fiction writers that seem to be popping up these days." He smiled and went on, "But a close and very dear friend of mine vouched for him and begged that I would hear him out."

Reilly continued, "I am assured by him that you will pass for my employer, and I don't doubt it. However, if, as Prescott says, the world must never know about it, you must do nothing unless I say so. Do you agree to this?"

"Of course," Bill said. "This is your territory and you know the ground rules better than I."

"Well said, sir. I believe we'll get along just fine. Now then, what is the plan of action?"

Prescott shifted closer to both men. "The date of the speech is November nineteenth. Is there a way we can have Mr. Scott observe your employer before that? Say, November seventeenth or eighteenth? It'll give him a chance to get acquainted with his mannerisms."

Reilly opened a small black appointment book and thumbed through it before saying. "Better we set the interview for the 10th at two pm. My employer will never question it because he tends to forget things told to him because of his . . . his . . . shall I say, times of forgetfulness? I suggest that you take a room in the Anthony House Hotel on 12th street. My assistant will greet and escort Bill to my office." "

As both time travelers nodded in agreement Reilly scratched his beard in thought.

"M . . . m . . .m, we have a bit of a problem. Mr. Lincoln is scheduled to leave the White House on the eighteenth and take a train to Gettysburg. That evening he is to attend a dinner and mingle with the many statesmen that will also be attending. I am not comfortable with Bill surrounded by so many of the president's friends and colleagues." He then slowly shook his head as he looked down at his feet.

"Sir," asked Prescott perplexed, "is there a problem with the plan?"

With a shrug Reilly said, "It's just that the President was to travel with," he looked up, closed his eyes tightly as he ticked off the names of the group who were to accompany Lincoln: "Secretary of State William Seward, Postmaster General Montgomery Blair, Interior Secretary John Usher, his personal secretaries John Hay and John Nicolay, several members of the diplomat corps, some foreign visitors, a Marine band, and a military escort." He opened his eyes and looked at both men. "Gentlemen, if I may make a suggestion?"

Bill looked at Prescott with raised eyebrows as he passed the question to him.

Prescott nodded, "Please, sir. Proceed."

"We have Mr. Lincoln come down with a cold."

"Pray tell, sir, what does that do for the mission?" asked Prescott.

"It would allow the others to travel down on the eighteenth as planned but I would have them believe that Mister Lincoln should stay in Washington and travel down the next day, thus riding alone."

"Can you persuade them to do so, sir?"

Reilly sat back and said with a grin, "I shall make the trip on the eighteenth more attractive by adding on a wine and spirits car with the White House covering all expenses." He nodded as he continued grinning, "Believe me, sirs, I know this group well and to be out of sight of their boss and their wives with the free flow of spirits around would entice them all to travel the day before the president does."

"Excuse me, Mister Reilly, "asked Bill, "but is there another train the next day?"

"Yes. The President takes standard scheduled transportation whenever possible. There will be a group of soldiers located at both ends of the car so the center section would be for us two only.

The trip is but two hours and ten minutes long and then we travel by coach for a short distance."

"Well," Prescott quipped, "it sounds as though the nineteenth is the day of your trip, gentlemen. What time do you leave the White House, Mister Reilly?"

"Eleven in the morning."

Prescott nodded and continued, "I need two hours to apply the makeup. Any suggestions as to where?"

"Indeed I do. I suggest you both check into the Anthony House Hotel on the nineteenth where you'll find reservations for you both. My assistant will greet and escort you both to my office. If, as you say, the President will be, ah, incapacitated, I shan't need to worry that he might call and there is no safer place to do this transformation than my office."

Bill and Prescott nodded in agreement, stood up and shook hands with the security man, then walked away into the sunny afternoon.

DATELINE: NOVEMBER 10, 1863 PLACE: RAILROAD CAR

11:00 A.M. on November 10 found Bill and Prescott traveling in an almost-empty 1860s railroad train. Although it was stuffy they kept the windows closed because every now and then hot embers from the coal-burning engine would fly into the train's interior along with the smoke. Old burn spots on the seats and rug kept them alert for fire. Bill thought the hissing of the overhead gas lamps were annoying whenever they sat in a station until they pulled out and the sound was replaced by the much louder clack clack of the steel wheels as they rolled over the small space between the separate rails.

A middle-aged conductor made his way through the cars, touching the seats briefly to steady himself from the sway of the train. He stopped and tipped his hat to them.

"About ten minutes 'till Washington, gentlemen," he said through a droopy white mustache, "Sorry about the delay. Some day they just haf'ta put up some fencing to keep them dang sheep off the tracks."

Bill and Prescott smiled at him, and the conductor shuffled through the door and into the next car.

"Prescott, I've been wondering: do you really think that the makeup will allow me to pass for the president?"

Prescott nodded, "I've had to use makeup kits supplied by our friends of the future a few times before and believe me, it will allow you to pass for Lincoln."

Bill shrugged and asked, "So is it more than grease paint and powder?"

Prescott sighed and nodded, "Much more, my friend. You see each kit is designed for a specific person to look like a specific person. In your case our friends have pictures and measurements of you and they worked on a model that was a duplicate of you. The kit uses a molecular changing formula that when applied transforms your facial muscles into a replica of Abraham Lincoln. It also contains synthetic hair for a beard and mustache. Please don't ask me how it works but the ends of the hair have a molecular additive that adheres to your skin."

"And how is this all removed?"

"A simple solution that when mixed with water and splashed on the face allows your normal facial muscles to take over and allow the real Bill Scott to return."

"And the beard and mustache?"

"Ahhh," answered Prescott, "I'm sure you'll have your shaving kit with you, correct?"

"Yes, I will. Is that how the beard and mustache is removed?"

Prescott grinned as he said, "Yes. But just think: if you ever wondered how you would look in a beard and mustache, this is your chance to see."

On arrival in the city, Bill was conscious that Washington had the same bad smells and smoke-darkened buildings as New York

City did. At the station, they caught a horse-drawn taxi over to the Anthony House Hotel on Twelfth Street. The newest time traveler found the cobblestone streets jarring and more than a match for the primitive suspension system of the carriage.

Three flights of stairs took them to their rooms. Prescott's room was across from Bill's and he said as he opened his door. "See you in a few minutes, Bill."

Bill opened his door to find overstuffed furniture and heavy curtains, which made the room gloomy. He opened the curtains, put his overnight bag on the high bed, and went to the washbasin, scooped up water and buried his face in it. After drying off, using a clean but thin towel, he took out a soft, brown leather attaché case that contained a small inkbottle, straight pens and paper in a pocket holder. He put his hands on his hips and said with a grin, "Tools of the time traveling writer's trade."

A light rap sounded on his door and he opened it to let Prescott in.

"How good are you with the straight quill pen?" asked Prescott as he pointed to them.

"Not good. Barely passable."

There was another knock at the door, and Bill opened it to find a slim, young, blond haired man in his mid-twenties with his hat in his hand.

"Mr. Scott?" he queried.

"Yes, I am Scott," Bill said.

The man offered his hand.

"O'Neil, John O'Neil. I'm with White House security."

They shook hands, and Bill turned toward Prescott and said, "Prescott Stevens, my editor. We are both with the *Chicago Times*."

"I understood that it'd be just you here for the interview," O'Neil said to Bill.

"Mr. Stevens is here to do some research on another article we are working on," Bill explained.

"Good. Mr. Reilly isn't one for surprises or changed plans," O'Neil said, with relief.

Prescott walked out the door past O'Neil and said, "In fact, I must go to my room and prepare for it now. Good luck, Bill. See you for dinner?"

"Dinner it is, Prescott. I'll knock on your door after my return."

O'Neil took a watch from his vest pocket. "Two past noon. We shall have to leave now to make our appointed time. Are you ready, sir?"

"I am. Just let me gather my notebook and pens." Bill repacked the writing materials and the two men left.

After another bone jarring carriage ride, Bill found himself in front of the White House of 1863. An armed Army officer checked O'Neil's credentials and waved them through. As they walked down the corridor, Bill was amazed by how much the building looked like the White House he had seen back, or rather forward, in the 1980s on a high school tour. O'Neil led the way upstairs and stopped in front of an unmarked door, knocked and waited. Reilly opened it. He had no jacket on, and Bill saw an 1860 Navy Colt pistol strapped under his arm. Reilly smiled broadly and greeted Bill like an old friend.

"Bill Scott! Damn, man, good to see you again," he said as he pumped his visitor's hand and slapped his back, allowing his hand to casually drop to the small of Bill's back. He guided his guest to a seat by gently grasping his arm. Bill didn't let on that he knew he had just been frisked by a pro. Reilly went over to a bar on one wall and picked up two glasses.

"Your pleasure, Bill?"

"Brandy, Kenneth."

"Brandy it is then. I must ask a favor, Bill. In our encounter with Mr. Lincoln, I ask that you call me Mr. Reilly."

"I understand," Bill responded. "What's the procedure?"

"Simple. At 2 P.M. I will take you into his private chamber, introduce you, and you follow his lead. You will have one half hour. Will that be good for your needs?"

"Hope so," Bill said. "I guess I just want to observe him. But believe me, this is fantastic! To meet one of our most famous presidents is almost beyond belief!"

Reilly handed Bill his drink and said, "Almost beyond belief? My God, man, it *is* beyond belief! I mean to have traveled back and forth in time. Why, it is like that French writer Jules Verne. He writes as though he has been in the future."

"Yes, he had, or rather, has, a fantastic imagination," Bill said.

Reilly sat down and selected a cigar from a box, offering one to his guest. Bill declined, but Reilly lit his and let out a long plume of smoke.

"Have you read any of his works, Bill?"

"Yes, I have, and I'm guessing you did too."

Reilly responded enthusiastically, "I got my hands on his notes of a future book he is working on, through a friend of mine, '*Twenty Thousand Leagues Under the Sea.'* Nothing but fantastic! Why, a vehicle that carries men under the oceans? Preposterous." He suddenly sat forward. "Or, is it preposterous? Does the future hold such an under-the-ocean carriage?"

Bill took a sip, and, looking perplexed, said, "I don't want to sound as if I'm speaking down to you, Kenneth, but do you really want to know such things?"

Reilly seized the opening. "I am by nature a curious man, Bill. I'm curious about you and Prescott. I'm curious about your mission. I'm curious about the people who sent you here. Why should I believe that Mr. Lincoln must deliver this speech? What happens if he doesn't deliver it?"

Bill started to say something, but Reilly put up his hand and stopped him. "As I said, Bill, I'm curious. But, after getting a glimpse of your world and hearing what Prescott had to say, I want to go along with your plan. I, too, believe that the speech must be made. I also feel that I'm doing my part now to preserve the United States of the future. And that overrides all of my curiosity. My duty calls from years after I am in the ground, and I shall answer that call. So if I ask for a little glimpse into your world, please, sir, indulge me." He drew on his cigar and exhaled through his nostrils, reminding Bill of a dragon.

Bill nodded. "You have a point, Kenneth. I'm not sure of the rules, if any, that this group has, but they did bring you into this plan. They needed you, so I will indulge you. You asked if an under-the-ocean vehicle exists in my time? Well, one not only exists, but it was an American named, John Holland who perfected it. And I've been on one many times."

Reilly's eyes opened as a child seeing birthday presents. "Lord, man, tell me what it's like. I mean to travel beneath the waves and not even get a drop of water on oneself? Amazing!"

Bill went on, "Amazing, true. But the submarine, as we call it, became a weapon of war. In fact, it's safe to say it's the ultimate weapon of war. It can't be seen or heard except by another submarine. It can sit on the bottom of the ocean and wait for months to do what it has been designed to do . . . wage war. We've become very good in the future at creating weapons that science fiction writers have only fantasized about. So you see my reluctance in enlightening you."

Reilly sat back in his chair. "I do, sir, I do. You must forgive me and my curiosity."

"Of course."

The security man looked at his pocket watch. "Finish your drink, Bill. The time is near."

They drained their glasses, and Reilly clipped his cigar before they left the room. He led the way up a flight of stairs then down a red-carpeted hallway towards a large white door guarded by two armed soldiers. The time traveler smiled to himself as he noted there were only fifteen paintings of past Presidents on the walls.

Bill was nervous as Reilly tapped on the door. A voice sounded from within.

"Yes?"

"Mr. President, it's Reilly."

"Come on in, Reilly."

Reilly opened the door and stood aside to allow Bill to enter. Abraham Lincoln, the sixteenth President of the United States, sat behind a desk that looked too small for him. He was signing some papers and looked up as the men entered. Bill's first thought was how large his hands and head seemed.

"Afternoon, Reilly," he said as he lowered his glasses until they dangled close to the end of his nose, "who've we got here?"

"Mr. President, this Mr. Bill Scott, a reporter from Chicago who wants to interview you for an article to run in next week's paper. I told him he has no more than one half hour because at three o'clock you are meeting with General Grant."

The president rose and offered Bill his hand. Lincoln smiled and said as he took in his height, "My, but you're also punished with having to look high an' low for garments that fit. I know what you go through in the everyday clothing and shoe store, sir, and I pity you."

Bill smiled at the natural warmth Lincoln exuded and was amazed how his own large hand seemed to disappear in the president's.

"Mr. President, I'd like to thank you in advance for allowing me a few minutes of your precious time."

"Nonsense. Sit down, sir. Coffee or somethin' a mite stronger perhaps?"

"No sir. But don't let that stop you."

"I can wait. Now, what paper is it that you write for?" President Lincoln asked.

"The Chicago Times, sir."

"Well then, shoot away," Lincoln, said as he sat back in his chair and crossed his arms.

The half hour flew by, thought Bill as he closed the door behind him. He walked past the soldiers and over to Reilly's office.

"How did the interview go?" Reilly wanted to know.

Bill was still tingling. "What a great man! He has such an easy-going attitude and speech. No wonder he goes down in history as one of the greatest men of all time."

"Yes, Bill, he is a great man. And I'm truly sorry that you have to help him through this. He has a great load on his shoulders and I can understand how it could get a strong man down. But, if as you say, history doesn't know of these trying times of his, well, I've done my job."

"You and your team have done a great job, Reilly, a great job."

They shook hands and Reilly said, "Let me get O'Neil to take you back to your hotel."

"No," Bill said. "I'm going to walk. I have so much to think about. It's been a great day and I want to savor it. Thank you."

"Prescott said he would brief you about the day of the switch. Do you feel comfortable with it, still?" Reilly asked.

"I do. I believe I can pull it off."

"You may need this pass during your stroll back," Reilly said as he scribbled on a White House memo pad, tore the sheet off and handed it to him. "See you soon, Bill."

"Good afternoon, Kenneth."

Bill walked back to his hotel thinking he truly was in a different world. The atmosphere had more than an odor to it; it had a feeling that, at any moment, something could happen. The streets were alive with squads of marching soldiers and cavalry. Bill noticed that cannons were placed at various spots throughout the city. He felt that the soldiers could pick him out as an outsider every time one looked at him. He turned a corner and saw a field cannon being set up in a small square and stopped to watch the men unlimber the weapon. As he watched a young captain approached him.

"You enjoy watching soldiers set up their pieces, mister?" he asked.

Caught off guard Bill nodded and answered, "Yes. Are you on maneuvers?"

The captain took a step back and put his hand on his pistol but didn't open the holster cover. "Why don't you show me some identification papers, mister?"

Bill was puzzled and mumbled, "Wha? Papers? Why?"

Now the Captain unbuttoned his holster and said, "You a Reb spy or somethin'? Ya' better show me some convincen' papers real fast, mister, and don't make no sudden moves."

Bill put his hands out as though to show he was weaponless. He saw the Captain looking at his writing case. "I'm a writer, Captain. I just had the good fortune to interview President Lincoln."

The military man eyed him as he said, "You interviewed Mr. Lincoln?"

Bill bent down slowly and removed his writing tablet and showed it to him. "Yes, I just left the White House this afternoon."

The captain looked at his notes and shrugged his shoulders, "Danged if this proves that you're not a Johnny Reb. I need to see some papers."

Bill reached inside his jacket with his left hand and removed the note Reilly gave him. He wasn't sure what it said and he was upset with himself for not reading it.

The Captain took and opened the folded paper as he stepped back a safe distance from Bill to read it. His eyes opened wide. He refolded it and returned it to Bill. He did a slight bow and smiled as he said, "Sorry Mr. Scott, but these here are hard times for all of us and I just can't take no chances. I do hope you understand." He pointed at the river, "Johnny Reb is right across the Potomac. Dang spies can be anywhere." He did a casual salute and walked back to his troops who were leaning against their gun while not being supervised by him.

Bill watched as the captain started shouting orders at his men and they got back to setting up the field gun. *Got to remember that Washington is in the front lines in this war, and I also have to read the note Reilly provided me,* he thought as he smiled, *I might be important.* He opened the note and read it. It was simple and to the point, ***"Let this man pass. He is a reporter, Mister William Scott. Ordered by White House Security Chief, Kenneth Reilly."*** It was signed with a very flourished Kenneth Reilly signature. *Looks like it's Reilly who's important.* Bill thought as he put the note away.

DATELINE: NOVEMBER 19, 1863 PLACE: THE WHITE HOUSE

The morning of November 19, 1863, was cold with overcast skies. Bill and Prescott were with Kenneth Reilly in a room with no windows. The security man stared at the tall man in the black coat and high hat, familiar to all as Lincoln-like attire. Prescott stood back and admired his handiwork. He passed a small hand mirror to Bill who looked at himself. He saw the sixteenth president of the United States staring back. Now he understood Reilly's shocked look.

Bill said, "Prescott, you've missed your vocation. You should have been a stage makeup artist."

"Believe me, Bill, the makeup kit I was given was made to have only one effect. To have you look like the President," Prescott responded.

Reilly spoke up. "Damn, man, he is the President's double!"

Bill fingered his fake beard and said, "Never had a beard . . . and now I know why. It's just not me. And thanks for the mole, Prescott. Nice touch, but it will come off later, right?"

"It's guaranteed."

Reilly checked his watch. "Let me hear you speak," he said to Bill.

"Fourscore and seven years ago . . ."

Reilly winced. "You have to speak in a higher tone of voice."

Prescott handed Bill a large handkerchief. "You have a cold, remember? Use the cloth as a cover for a deeper voice."

Bill covered his mouth and spoke a few more words.

Reilly nodded and said, "Better. And I'm going to keep everyone away from you. A few key people know of this. They are watching over Mr. Lincoln who is in one of his states just as Prescott predicted he'd be. The fewer people who know the better. Keep reading your speech, and I'll let on that you are under pressure to put it to memory. We'd better move out to the carriage." He turned to Prescott, "I'm afraid you have to stay behind, Prescott."

"I understand. I'll wait at the hotel. Good luck gentlemen."

Reilly opened the door, and Bill, in his Lincoln guise, started to follow.

Prescott caught up with them and whispered to Bill, "Walk tall, sir, you are the President of the United States of America. Make all who see you, believe it."

Bill walked purposefully out the door and climbed into the carriage. Reilly climbed in next to him. As they drove off, Bill held the speech so it shielded his face. He turned to Reilly, "What are you going to tell Lincoln about this when he reads of it in the papers?"

Reilly lit a cigar. "I'm going to tell him he did a wonderful job today. You know, Bill, being with a person who has an illness, who you really like, makes you a great liar. He doesn't think we know he has these bouts of depression, and we make believe that we don't know. I'm not here to change him, just to protect and serve him and the Union." Bill nodded agreement, and they rode on.

The journey was short, bumpy and chilly. Bill was nervous about his upcoming speech, not so much about the speech, but rather in meeting General Grant and being an important part of history. At the train station, the military guard surrounded him as they walked to the waiting train. A man dressed in a red jacket and black pants with a broad red stripe down the legs stood tall with a large smile as he motioned to the car that was empty of all passengers and ready for President Lincoln and his guard. No sooner had they all taken their seats then the whistle blew announcing its departure. Bill looked out the clean windows and saw the trainman still smiling as he waved his hat and he smiled and waved back. The time traveler grinned to himself as he thought, *someone is going to have a nice story for their grandchildren.*

The train ride took two hours and Bill was thrilled to just sit back and look out the window at the scenery going past. He had a cup of hot tea and some cookies from another trainman who deftly walked through the rocking car.

Once at their station Bill and Reilly entered a horse drawn coach as a group of Cavalry took over escort duty and led the way.

Reilly was drifting off into a nap when the officer of the guard rapped on the side of the carriage. "Gettysburg, Mr. President."

Reilly was awake in an instant and out of the carriage. He held the door for Bill.

"This way, Mr. President," the security man said as he pointed toward the sea of Army tents on an open plain. Broad, flat boards acted as bridges over mud puddles. Wet laundry hung on ropes tied from trees, and it was so cold that Bill could see his breath. The area had the smell of troops who worked hard and didn't have a chance to wash well. There was also, the now familiar, odor of horses along with beef being slaughtered for food.

Funny, Bill thought, *when you see pictures of the famous meeting, it looks gray and colorless, and here in person, it is gray and colorless.*

Soldiers emerged from their tents to see what the fuss was. When they realized it was their President, they started to cheer him. Bill was startled and looked to Reilly for guidance.

Reilly gave a sly nod and said in a low voice, "Wave to them, sir. They are seeing their President. Give them a danged good wave. Show them confidence."

Bill smiled and waved to the gathering crowd. Sergeants stepped between the soldiers and Bill, shouting for them to stay at ease and quiet down. They fell silent and watched in awe as history unfolded before them.

The officer in charge stopped at a tent larger than the others, and a heavyset figure stepped out putting his hat on. Bill tried to hide his excitement at meeting General Ulysses S. Grant, victor of the Civil War. Grant stepped forward and saluted his Commander-In-Chief. Bill answered it with a snappy salute back and offered his hand. Grant's eyebrows rose, and he smiled as he shook Bill's hand.

"Mr. President. Good to see you again, sir."

Bill coughed, cleared his throat and in a deep voice answered, "Good to see you too, General. How have you been? This is nasty weather."

"I've been good, sir. Nice of you to ask and yes, the weather is nasty. Are you coming down with a cold?"

"I am, sir," the impostor said. "But how can I complain when I see the field conditions that you and the troops must endure."

"As you know, Mr. President, we shall be marching in a short time, and if it goes as I plan, we shall be in warmer weather soon."

Bill smiled reassuringly. "I'm sure it'll go your way, General. Pray Godspeed to you and your men."

The officer in charge stepped in and said, "Excuse me, sirs, but the scheduled time of Mr. Lincoln's speech is approaching, and we feel that the weather shouldn't be tempted. There are a few of them photographer fellas here who would like some pictures for their papers and they promise to be swift."

After a few flashes, the cameramen were having a hard time igniting the illuminating powder because of the light mist from the clouds. Grant took Bill's elbow and said, "Come, Mr. President, there are newspaper reporters from the four corners of the world awaiting your words."

The General and the President walked toward a small wooden stage sheltered by an awning. In front of the stage were wooden seats for the reporters. It was apparent that Bill would be on the platform alone when Grant, the officer, and Reilly stopped at the bottom of the three steps going up to the stage.

Bill went up the steps and looked out at the audience of reporters, soldiers and congressmen. The reporters had their notebooks at the ready. As thunder rumbled overhead, Bill took out the notes he had been given by Prescott. As he looked at them, it suddenly hit him that he would be performing one of the most historic moments in history. What he would say now would help determine the future of the United States of America, and in many ways, the world.

He put the notes back in his pocket. As he began to give the famous speech, Reilly realized that Scott didn't have to disguise his voice. The tremble in his delivery let the crowd of people know they heard words that would change history. The man speaking them didn't need to read them as they truly were coming from his heart.

When the speech ended, the silence was profound. Bill took a last look at the stunned audience and slowly walked off the stage. Only then did the crowd go wild. They stood and cheered, and many had tears in their eyes. Bill had just recited the Gettysburg Address the same way Lincoln would have. He felt drained. Grant shook his hand long and hard.

"Mr. President," the general said with feeling, "the world will learn of your words and join our worthy cause. You, sir, have inflicted a grave wound on the rebel armies."

Bill nodded his thanks. He turned to Reilly and said, "Mr. Reilly, we have a long journey ahead of us, both as a nation and as travelers back to Washington. I suggest we start while the weather holds."

Reilly replied in a low voice, "I agree, Mr. President."

They walked back to the carriage through knots of soldiers standing with their hats in their hands. The ride back was quiet.

Later, a clean-faced Bill sat in his hotel room having a drink with Reilly and Prescott.

Reilly raised his glass. "Hail to the chief. You were masterful, sir. I do feel all believed your performance."

Bill threw back his drink and poured another. "I shook hands with so many boys who are going to die. I looked into their eyes and saw hope. Hope in me! Me . . . a make believe President. They looked at me as a person who will hopefully bring this war to an end. I feel . . . dirty. As if I'm letting them down."

Prescott patted him on his shoulder and said, "Don't berate yourself. This is what it's all about. Getting a chance to keep history on its correct track. It's the same history, but with a personal touch now that you're a part of it. You did a great job, Bill and I congratulate you. Shall we go home?"

Bill nodded yes; Reilly finished his drink, stood, and offered his hand. "Gentlemen, thank you for the most wonderful adventure of my life. Will I see you again?"

Prescott shook his hand. "No, we will go back to New York, and then I'm off to New Jersey and retirement."

"And I'm off to my own times," Bill said as he shook Reilly's hand. "But this has been my most fantastic adventure and I thank you both."

Reilly nodded in agreement.

The next morning, Bill knocked on Prescott's door and one moment later he opened it, half dressed.

"Good morning, Bill. Am I late?"

"No," said Bill. "I am taking the liberty of staying another day in Washington. I want to take it all in before I return. Do you mind traveling alone or do you wish to extend your stay as well?"

Prescott answered with a soft smile, "No, my friend. It's time for me to go home. Our job is done here and my sister awaits me. You stay and enjoy yourself. You deserve it."

As the men were parting, Bill looked him in the eyes and said, "Prescott, will I see you again?"

Prescott shook his head. "No, I don't think so. I want to stay in my own time. I want to see my family and maybe do some painting."

Bill left the hotel and went out into the busy streets of Washington. He was suddenly aware of how relaxed he was. He truly felt a part of the 1800s as he hailed an open carriage and deftly climbed up and took his seat. The driver looked back over his shoulder, "Where to, sir?"

Bill replied with a big grin, "Nowhere in particular. I just want to take a sightseeing tour of the area."

The man relaxed the reins, lit his clay pipe, and allowed the horse to walk slowly down the street. Bill felt great satisfaction that he had pulled off the job that could have come only from a novel.

But here I am, he thought, *back in the time I've always dreamed about, looking at buildings being built that are more than one hundred years old in my time.*

The carriage turned down the tight streets of Georgetown and along the wider main streets. In the bright daylight, people strolled past quaint row houses and small restaurants along the cobblestone streets. As usual, the smoke poured from most of the chimneys as people prepared food. Bill noticed that the air seemed especially foul today and many people had their noses covered.

The driver said over his shoulder, "Poor luck for us, sir. The wind brings the Potomac's smell this way today."

Bill remembered the river was polluted at this time.

The carriage casually turned a corner, and he suddenly spotted Reilly sitting in an open-air restaurant having mid-morning coffee.

Bill was about to stop the carriage when he saw that Reilly was not alone. He was with another man and the difference was striking. The man was dressed fashionably with long hair, a short pointed beard and mustache while Reilly wore a nondescript three-piece suit. The man was good-looking and quite animated.

I told him that I wouldn't be seeing him again, Bill thought as he decided to keep going, but looked back. Reilly's companion seemed familiar, *but* he thought, *that's impossible. I can count on one hand the people I've met in this time.*

The cab turned down another street, and Bill's attention drifted at the sight of children running beside a marching military band leading more recruits to their barracks.

Washington and History passed by as the cab plodded slowly along.

DATELINE: NOVEMBER 13, 2011   PLACE: THE 1800 CLUB, NEW YORK CITY

The next day Bill was back at the club. He sat behind the large desk that once belonged to Prescott, sipped coffee and munched on toast with peanut butter. He was tired from the long Washington to New York train and carriage trip and looked forward to sleeping that evening in the large Federal-style bed that came with the job.

He thought about calling Charlene and telling her about his new job then shrugged it off. *It's over. Forget her.* He sat straight up as he realized he hadn't thought of her in days. He smiled as he finished his coffee. *I'll trot over while she's at work and grab my stuff. Heck, maybe I'll even leave her a note.*

After breakfast, he took a book on Lincoln from the huge library and with a magnifying glass studied a photograph of the President at Gettysburg as he stood outside an Army tent. Bill chuckled as he remembered how he had tripped over one of the tent-peg ropes. Every soldier around and even a general had rushed to help him.

He returned the book to the shelf and scanned over some of the other titles. He stopped at one, *Lincoln: Birth, Life and Death of a Great Statesman.* Bill took it over to his desk and began to thumb through the pages. Grainy black-and-white photos illustrated the large coffee-table book. He stopped to look at himself once more outside the tent and smiled again.

As he turned the pages in the section titled, "Death of a President," a small photo caught his attention. He stared at it and reached for the magnifying glass. It was the man Reilly had coffee with as he rode by in the carriage. Bill's eyes went wide. The caption read. "John Wilkes Booth shot President A. Lincoln on April 14, 1865."

He gasped as he thought, *John Wilkes Booth! Why was Reilly having coffee with him? Doesn't he know . . .? No, wait! Of course, he doesn't know. I've got to go back and tell him.* He sat back and continued to stare at the photo. *Tell him what? That his friend is going to kill his boss? No, I've got to do some more research on both men before I act.*

Thirty minutes later Bill sat on the floor, books strewn about.

"Prescott, where are you now that I need you?" he muttered. "Man, I have to think about this." He scrambled to the desk and grabbed a pencil and some paper as he thought, *All right, let me make a list of all this.*

#1: Lincoln has spells of depression; the top level of his Security Service knows it and covers it up.

#2: Reilly knows John Wilkes Booth, Lincoln's killer.

#3: Or, Reilly <u>doesn't</u> know that Booth is planning to kill the president.

#4: Is Booth using Reilly to get information about the President so he can kill him?

"Or #5: Reilly knows that Booth is going to kill the President and is in on it."

Bill's mind continued to race. *Either way I have to handle this carefully. I don't want to go back and start being seen by Reilly in case he is in on the assassination, so I have to pick the right time to be there.*

He looked at the book and read again, *John Wilkes Booth shot President A. Lincoln on April 14, 1865.* He slammed it closed. "That's the time. That's when I have to be there," Bill said to himself.

He went down to the club's changing rooms and selected a typical mid-eighteen hundreds three-piece dark brown suit. After he put on the heavily starched white shirt he struggled to tie a nice and puffy cravat around the stiff collar. Finished, he held the dark brown cravat in place by piercing it with a gold stickpin. Bill put the end of a gold pocket watch chain into the vest's third buttonhole, draped it across his middle and slipped the watch into his vest pocket. He then put on a pair of high-top brown shoes and buttoned them. He looked in the long mirror and said to himself, "Well you look the part, but are you really ready for this?" He nodded at his reflection and with a shrug added, "Well you better be because you're on your own."

Back upstairs he opened the door at the rear of the den and stepped out onto the landing. He took out his Time Frequency Modulator and after entering his password, 'President', added April 14, 1865, 7:00 A.M. Bill walked down the stone steps, his only companion was his shadow supplied by the wall-mounted gas lamps.

Once at the first landing he pressed the 'Activate' button on his TFM and opened the security door.

DATELINE: APRIL 14, 1865 7:00 A.M. PLACE: THE 1800 CLUB'S GARDEN, NEW YORK CITY

Bill walked briskly through the garden hardly taking a moment to linger in the luscious setting. Once outside the gate he locked it behind himself and walked to the corner.

He spotted three carriages standing on the next corner and headed towards them. The driver of the first cab tipped his hat to reveal a full head of red hair that matched his full beard and mustache. He smiled as he asked, "Cab, sir?"

"Yes," answered Bill nervous that the man would see through his disguise of a person from 2011 rather than 1865.

The man's smile relaxed the time traveler as he said, "And where is it that you'ld like ta go, sir?"

"Um, well I need to catch a train to Washington, D.C."

The driver nodded, "Then it's the ferry to New Jersey so ya can catch the train south."

"Sounds right to me."

"Sit back an' relax and me an' Diana will get ya there shortly."

Bill sat back as the driver called out, "C'mon Diana we got a ferry boat ride coming up."

The carriage pulled away from the curb and Bill realized that because of his time at the 1800 Club he felt almost at home in this time. The ride to the ferry took them across every type of road that New York City had. The steel wheel rims slipped and bounced off the cobble stone streets followed by a sharp dip as the wheel bounced through a section of missing cobblestones. Next they sent a chattering through the carriage as the driver rode along a street or two made up of wooden boards and then the sudden quietness of a dirt packed street. The driver slowed and Bill saw that he turned down Courtland Street along with dozens of cabs, freight carrying wagons, and single horse and rider traffic all converging at the end of the street. A large building with wide open doors faced them and he was perplexed when the driver pulled over to the curb.

The answer came as the driver called down, "Sir, ya have no need of me anymore as the train station is right where the ferry docks."

Bill stepped out as the driver said, "Twenty-five cents, sir".

Bill paid him along with a tip and waved goodbye as he walked towards the building.

The two sidewalks had about thirty people all heading towards the open doors. As the goal was to be the first on and thus the first off, the wagons, taxies and cabs all merged with more than one profanity spoken along with the bumping of wheels as the larger wagons sideswiped the smaller out of their way.

Bill grinned as he thought, *It's the same in this time as in my time. Everyone wants to be first. The only thing different is the one or two horsepower of this time versus the much larger horsepower of the cabs and trucks of my time.*

Bill paid the two cents fare at the small window of the cashier's booth and entered the large hollow ferryboat. As he and all of his fellow travelers headed towards the front of the boat he saw that the all of the drivers sat with their hand or foot on the mechanical brake on their vehicle to prevent any rolling if the crossing is a rough one.

A sudden blast of the ferryboat's whistle warned everyone to hold tight as she pulled away from the slip.

Once out in the open water heading towards New Jersey the water became choppy but the cool fresh air was clean and the smells and sounds of the city was left behind.

There were lots of large and small boats plying the waterway and Bill saw many accidents averted at the last moment. They were powered by wind, steam and oar and all had one goal: to make money by taking people, wagons and carriages across the waterway. The strangest he saw was what was known as a 'horseboat'. The boat was carrying five one-horse wagons and was powered by six mules walking on a treadmill, which was connected by a gear to paddle wheels.

Eight minutes later they docked and all the wagons, carriages and horsemen scampered to be the first off. A sign pointed the way to the train depot and in five minutes Bill had purchased a ticket to Washington D.C. According to a large blackboard on the wall the train would leave at 9:00 A.M. and arrive in Washington D.C. at 4:15 P.M.

Bill joined the other passengers sitting in the large waiting room as a wall-mounted clock ticked off the minutes.

Everyone watched as an elderly, thin man slid a tall ladder along the wall until he was beneath the chalkboard. He then went up the ladder and printed in large letters, ***Train Number 609 leaves N.J. for W.D.C. From Track 3.***

He got down just as a man dressed in a blue uniform with a hat that sported an emblem which was too far away to be seen cupped his hands and called out, "Train 609 now boarding on track 3." He then went to a door marked Track 3 and threw it open before quickly stepping out of the way of the rushing crowd.

Bill joined the crowd and saw a train letting off a steady stream of steam as a man dressed in coveralls was actually oiling some of its drive gear. The time traveler stepped up the wooden stool in front of the door of car number four and took a window seat.

He shook his head, *This is fantastic! Getting a train ride in the mid-1800s.* He grinned as he shook his head. *Problem is I have no one to tell.*

The train was mostly wood with small glass windows and overhead hissing gas lamps. The seats were upholstered in horsehair filled dark blue corduroy. A dark green rug ran down the center aisle and each aisle seat had a steel handgrip to assist a passenger as they walked down the aisle while the train drove on.

Ten minutes later the train's whistle sounded and five minutes later the large wheels started to turn as the train went down the track.

A tall slim young man dressed in a blue uniform and hat walked slowly through the rocking train punching tickets.

Bill got nervous as he felt the conductor, who saw hundreds of people a week would easily spot him as an outsider.

The man stopped and took his ticket before saying, "Thank you, sir. Enjoy your trip in Washington." He then moved on to the passenger behind a relieved Bill Scott.

Bill looked out the window as the scenery flew by and was surprised when he heard, "Washington D.C. next and last stop."

It was then that he realized he had fallen asleep. He suddenly felt completely relaxed. *If I fell asleep I'm pretty sure I feel like I'm one of them.*

At the station was a group of carriages many of which were cabs and Bill flagged on edown.

"Where to sir? Asked the cab driver.

"The Anthony House please."

Fifteen minutes later Bill was washing his face in his room. He sat back in one of the two easy chairs the room had as he thought, *I'm not going to take any chances of being spotted by Reilly before tonight. I'm going to wait right here.*

Bill looked at his pocket watch. *6:30 and the sun sets at 7:31.*
I'm going to catch a cab and blend in with the crowd.

He caught a cab and in ten minutes was deep in the crowd at
Ford's Theater buying tickets. He went into the lobby where he
heard other theatergoers saying excitedly that the President would
be there for the evening's performance. As he went in to find his
seat, he looked up to his right saw the empty presidential box
draped in the flag of the Union.

Bill's seat was in the downstairs center, and he looked up again
at the presidential box. It was still empty. He continued to
familiarize himself with the theater, noting the exits, and spotted a
door on his level marked 'To Balcony.'

The crowd was patient as they waited to see if the president
would come in before the curtain parted. Suddenly he heard
murmuring from the back of the house. The sound increased as
more people turned around and whispered, "The President and
Mrs. Lincoln have arrived."

The audience began to applaud as President and Mrs. Lincoln
were seated in their box. One moment later the President stood and
graciously bowed.

Bill saw Reilly and a uniformed guard in the open doorway behind the seated Lincolns. Knowing that the assassin would strike at 10:15 he sat through the play until it was time for him to act.

He shook his head as he remembered Prescott saying: '*Our job is not to change history, but rather keep it on course.*'

Bill told himself, *I'm not trying to change history I just need to know was it Booth who did the shooting and was he allowed passage into the box by Reilly?*

Excusing himself, Bill left his seat and headed toward the balcony door. He mentally shook his head at the lack of security when he found it unlocked. The time traveler went quickly and quietly up the poorly lit carpeted stairs. Opening the door onto the balcony, he saw another box next to the one in which the Lincolns sat. Its deep red curtains were half opened, showing it was empty.

He stepped inside and peeked around to see the rear of the presidential box. He saw the guard standing in front of the curtain. *Reilly must be inside,* he thought. His mind began some quick calculations, and he thought, *should I confront Reilly? What will I say? What if I somehow screw up history?*

Then he heard Reilly addressing the guard. "If you need to have a latrine break, this is the time. Then I'd like you to tell Lieutenant Pearson that I want a few more men up here. I just heard a rumor that there are some bad elements in town tonight."

Bill heard the soldier walk away briskly and go down the stairs.

It's time, he thought. *I can't just stand here. I've got to confront him.*

He stepped out of the box and walked toward the President's box. Suddenly Reilly was in front of him, pistol drawn, cocked and aimed at Bill's head.

Reilly blurted out, "You? I had a feeling there was someone in that box, but not you! What are you doing here?"

"Just lower the pistol and we can talk," Bill said.

"Not on your life. Hands high. Walk over there and turn around," Reilly said, gesturing toward an out-of-the-way corner.

Bill did as he was told, and Reilly patted him down. "No concealed weapon," Reilly said, as he kept his pistol on Bill. "Why are you here? I thought your mission was over a couple of years ago?"

"That mission was over. This may not even be a mission. Tell me about John Wilkes Booth," Scott responded.

Reilly's eyes narrowed. "How did you find out about him? Were you following me?"

Bill shook his head no, "Just by chance. You met with him in a restaurant the day I was supposed to leave Washington. His face looked familiar. It was. He is the man who killed Abraham Lincoln."

Reilly was suddenly jubilant. "So, the plan works! The world is done and finished with that self-righteous, depressed, poor excuse of a man."

Incredulous, Bill said, "But you are Lincoln's protector! Why do you wish him harm?"

With some eagerness, Reilly began to explain, "I don't wish him harm. Other factions do. I intend to bring them to justice after the deed is done. I see this as a chance to strengthen the States. When the President is shot, Booth has no way out but past me. I'll shoot him during his getaway and that shot will be a signal for others to take over Washington for its own protection. After all, the people don't know how many other criminal elements are in on the act. They'll believe anything we tell them."

"But why? I thought you were all for a great democracy. Why turn this into a dictatorship?"

Reilly leaned toward Bill and said fervently, "Because I want the United States of America to be the one and only power on the face of the Earth. I want all other governments to prostrate themselves before us. We shall stop all tyranny in the world and there will be one central seat of power . . . Washington!"

Still trying to make sense of what he was hearing, Bill continued, "How would you do that? I mean England and France would never stand for that. They'll join forces and invade and defeat you."

Reilly smiled. "Very simple. The submarine! Thanks to your information, I've tracked down Mr. John Holland and asked him of his plans for an undersea craft. He was quite enthusiastic to share them with me. I told him to keep the meeting a secret and that I would see about getting the U.S. Navy to finance it. I have friends in the Navy who are quite willing to back it."

"But his submarine won't be ready until 1893, that's still twenty-eight years away," Bill replied.

Reilly grinned. "In your time, perhaps. But from what I understand from your mission, history can be changed. And by getting Mr. Holland the funds he needed years earlier, we can shortly have a fleet of undetectable, quiet craft, and, to quote you, 'the ultimate weapon of war.'"

Bill shook his head and responded, "Absolute power corrupts absolutely."

"Well said, sir, and now I'm afraid you will have to die as one of the gang of hoodlums." He cocked the pistol at the same time a muffled shot erupted from behind Bill. The crowd screamed and Reilly smiled again. "Right on time. The President is dead! Goodbye Mr. Scott . . ."

Bill lunged at him the same moment a shot rang out. He grasped Reilly around the waist, only to feel no resistance. Both men fell to the floor, and then Bill's eyes were even with the security man's. The bullet hole in Reilly's forehead puzzled Bill for a moment.

Then he saw someone wearing brown boots step out quickly from a nearby box. Holding a smoking pistol was O'Neil. He looked down at Bill and asked, "Are you hurt, Mr. Scott?"

"N . . . no . . . no, just shook up. Did you hear everything?"

The young security man was already turning away. "Everything. I can't believe Reilly was a traitor. I must see to the President."

Three hectic days later Bill and O'Neil were having a drink at a local tavern.

"Mr. Scott, what you tell me is fantastic," O'Neil said. "Extremely hard to believe, yet all you say comes true."

Bill nodded in agreement. "True, all right. It's hard for me, too. I'm new at this. But I'm puzzled. Why were you at the theater?"

"I thought it strange," O'Neil confided. "The President and Mrs. Lincoln were going to the theater, and Reilly gave me the day off. Not the way he usually did things. But I had already become suspicious. Mr. Reilly seemed to be spending a considerable amount of time with a new group of friends. Many were officers in the military, but others were more doubtful. He met with them at their homes or clandestinely. He had taught me many ways to spot a dangerous fellow, and he started to exhibit the same traits."

O'Neil sipped his drink. "So I started to follow him. He met many times with Mister John Holland, a cheerful fellow and not part of this conspiracy as far as I can tell. One day, by accident, I saw some plans on Reilly's desk with Mister Holland's name at the bottom. They were drawings for an ocean-going ship of destruction. I once asked him about Holland, and he became furious. Not really like him at all."

Bill raised his glass. "I'm glad you did. And because the public has enough grief at this time, you decided to let them think Reilly was shot by Booth?"

O'Neil spread his hands and shrugged. "What good would it have done to expose him? I'll have the officers quietly removed from their posts and let it all die down. Do you agree with my tactics, Mr. Scott?"

"I do, Mr. O'Neil, I surely do. You're hitting the ground running as far as I can see."

"A strange saying, sir, but I take it as a compliment."

Bill slapped him on his back and said with a smile, "It is. You'll go far in this business."

O'Neil shook his head. "No, sir. I'm leaving the security business."

"Leaving? But why?"

O'Neil leaned back in his chair. "Too much intrigue and too many late nights. I want to enjoy my family. My wife and I have a six-month-old baby girl, and I want to be there with my wife and watch her grow up."

Bill nodded, "I understand. Is there anything I can do for you?"

"Such as?"

"Such as a holiday in New York . . . in my time?"

O'Neil shook his head. "No, thank you anyway, Mr. Scott. But I do believe my wife would not want to see a change in me, and I do not want to tempt myself to see things I should not, as Mr. Reilly did."

"Wise of you, sir. But will you take a little advice? Purely for the sake of your wife and child?" Bill offered.

"And what would that be, sir?"

"There's a man looking for advice and financial assistance. His name is James Plimpton."

"Is Mr. Plimpton in the security business?"

"No, Mr. Plimpton has an idea for a transportation system that goes on your feet. His design has four wheels, rather than the standard two, and is much, much easier to use than the old style.

They will be called roller skates, and believe me, they will catch on, and you and your family will be set for life. He resides in Medford, Massachusetts and should be easy for you to look up."

O'Neil made some notes on a small pad then finished his drink and stood up. The men shook hands, and O'Neil asked, "Mr. Scott, will we meet again?"

Bill answered, "No, Mister O'Neil, I don't think so, but you never can tell."

DATELINE: NOVEMBER 17, 2011 11:30 A.M.   PLACE: THE 1800 CLUB, NEW YORK CITY

Back in his club's den in New York City, Bill sat at his computer while a snowstorm raged outside. A knock at the Time Portal door grabbed his attention.

"Prescott?" Bill mumbled as he happily crossed the room, slid the key into the lock and swung the door wide open. "Pres . . ."

A tall young man in his mid-twenties wearing a one-piece light blue suit stood there. He was a clean-shaven, dark haired man about Bill's height. He smiled and his blue eyes twinkled as he offered a hand to Bill.

"Bill Scott, I'm Edmund Scott. I'm from 2066 and very pleased to meet you."

Bill was surprised but not shocked. He shook the stranger's hand and said, "Same here, Mr. Scott. Is it a coincidence that we share the same last name, or are we related?"

"We are related, Bill, I am your grandson."

Now Bill *was* shocked, but he beamed at meeting his future relative. "Damn! This gets better and better. Did they just recruit you to meet me, or what?"

"No, I've been a part of the Time Watchers program since I was eighteen years old. You can say it runs in the family. After you, it was a natural selection for us Scotts."

"Come in . . .err . . . Ed . . . err . . . Edmund. What do I call you?"

The young man entered the room and answered, "My friends call me Edmund, and I you? Grandpa . . ."

"Don't! Stop right there," Bill interrupted. "It's obvious that I get married, but I don't want to know everything. I'd prefer to let it just happen. And please call me Bill." He closed the door behind Edmund. "Would you like a drink, Edmund? Coffee, tea or whatever?"

"No thanks, Bill. I was selected to be your contact, and I waited until you finished your first mission. You did great. I'm proud to be a Scott."

"Lots of credit has to go to Prescott Stevens. It was his call."

"Mr. Stevens is a legend in our time and, believe me, you have just gained a lot of respect from the time watcher's group. You are a perfect successor for him." Edmund put a hand out to steady himself on the desk. "Whoa . . . little dizzy for a second. The air, you know. I can't stay long, not used to it. Maybe over time . . . "

Bill helped him into a chair. "Stay still and breathe slowly. I'll get you some water."

"No, no thanks. They told me the water from this era would upset me. I'll just sit a second."

"Right," Bill said, "But I'm curious. Are you here to give me an assignment or just to let me see my future family?"

Edmund smiled as he rubbed his temples. "Just to introduce myself and let you know that we of the future, appreciate your work. As for an assignment, nothing yet." He took a slow breath, "There is a hint of Theodore Roosevelt swerving off course, but it may be nothing. We are sending a probe back to investigate the possibility and will let you know."

He started to stand up, wobbled, and Bill went to help him.

Edmund said slowly, "I'm okay, Bill. I just have to come for short visits until I become more . . . more, acclimated to your air. But for now . . . "

They shook hands, and then Bill hugged him. "Do families do that in your time?"

Edmund smiled. "They do. I'll see you soon, Grandpa Bill."

Bill gave him a good-natured punch on the arm and walked him to the door. "Edmund, let me just ask you this. Is there a Charlene Greene anywhere in your family line?"

"No," Edmund said, his face in thought, "never heard that name before. Should I know her?"

Bill smiled and answered, "No, just wondering. Now, take care of yourself, you young whippersnapper."

Bill closed the door, as a tap on the den's door drew his attention.

"Come in, Matt."

The door opened, and Matt entered. "The guests are seated, sir" Bill nodded as he looked in the full-length mirror and straightened his cravat. "What's on the menu tonight, Matt?"

"Roast pork chops, carrots, corn, mashed potatoes, cornbread and brown gravy, sir."

"Excellent. Be down in a minute. Thanks, Matt."

Bill turned back to his computer and looked at the results of the subject he had punched into Google. The text read, "In the late 1800s, James Plimpton invented what became the modern-day roller skates. His small company received an infusion of cash from John O'Neil, who became a partner in the firm. Both men lived to ripe old ages and saw their company grow to be at the top of the roller skate kingdom and worth millions of dollars." Along with the text was a black and white photo of O'Neil smiling at Bill from across the years.

Bill smiled and closed the laptop. He put his jacket on and walked toward the stairs as the storm outside continued to howl. He caught his reflection in a dark window and wondered what his next mission would be. *Boy,* he thought, *I'd love to meet Teddy Roosevelt.*

The Theodore Roosevelt Mission

DATELINE: 1898 PLACE: CUBA

A bullet ricocheted off a rock and dug itself into a tree trunk, almost hitting a butterfly. In a foxhole beneath the same tree, an army private noticed that the butterfly didn't even react to the near miss.

Guess being scared is only for us humans; he thought and quickly ducked his head as another shot whipped past his ear. He didn't see as the butterfly flew off and perched itself on another tree close to three uniformed men in a large shell hole. They held an unfolded map, studied it, and looked around as though trying to orient themselves. A slim, gray-haired man wearing U.S. Army Captain's bars gestured to the group's right flank.

"Sir, I believe the Spaniards are up that hill," he said.

All three ducked in unison as a burst of rifle fire tore through the dirt in front of them.

"Damn close," muttered Colonel Theodore Roosevelt, as he wiped the dirt off his glasses. "Damn close."

The third man, a lieutenant, shook his head in disagreement and pointed to a spot on the map. "Sirs, with all due respect, I do believe the enemy is on our left flank."

The colonel squinted up the hill. "It's their damned smokeless gunpowder," he said. "They're picking us off one by one and we can't even see where they are. Isn't fair."

Another burst followed by an explosion put the three officers deeper into their makeshift foxhole. Roosevelt looked perplexed, while the two other officers were close to an argument as each expressed his theory of the enemy's position.

A runner suddenly jumped into the already-tight hole and breathlessly reported: "Message for you, Colonel Roosevelt. Captain Lewis spotted the Spaniards straight ahead and up on San Juan Hill. He requests your troops take it as soon as possible to relieve the pressure on his flank."

Roosevelt looked at his map, then forward to the top of the hill. "Tell Captain Lewis I'll attack as soon as I can, Corporal."

"Yes, sir," the runner said as he crawled out of the hole and scurried off to deliver the message.

Through the smoke of battle, the three officers tried to make out the hilltop.

"It's going to be a tough one, Colonel," said the captain.

"That it is," replied Roosevelt through tight lips, "that it is."

The Lieutenant looked at him. "Sir, if we can get an artillery piece to fire on the hilltop to keep their heads down, we might be able to pull it off."

The heavyset colonel brushed dirt off his tan uniform jacket and said with a grimace, "There are no artillery pieces ready in our sector and to attack straight up the hill would be sheer suicide. No, I'm afraid we'll have to wait until it gets dark."

The Captain sat in the bottom of the hole and lit a cigar. "It won't be dark for hours yet. But we can't just go up the hill and attack their front. We'll be mowed down. I hope Lewis can hold out until nightfall."

A butterfly skimmed over their heads and startled the three men.

"Don't blame the little critter," said Roosevelt as he wiped dust off his boots. "If I had wings I might do the same."

The two officers looked at their commander and wondered if he really would fly off if he could.

DATELINE: JULY 9, 2066 PLACE: HISTORY TRACKING CENTER, NEW YORK CITY

As the person in charge of this mission, John Hyder sat at the head of a long, mahogany table. The mid-thirties, blond-haired man scratched his long, gray-flecked sideburns nervously as he activated the hologram brought back by the butterfly probe. The rest of the history watchers team sat waiting to see why he had summoned the group meeting.

Hyder mentally checked the group in: Joseph Sergi, tall at six-feet six-inches with long dark hair that was always in his eyes and made all think he was much younger than his 40 years of age sat on Hyder's left and white-haired Maryellen Muldey sat next to him. She was the eldest of the group and proud of her sixty-two years. At Hyder's right sat raven-haired Alexis Shuntly whose green eyes peered at him through thick glasses that made her look older than her forty-five years of age. Finally, there was Jerry Sullivan, who perpetually smiled and cleaned his spotless eyeglasses. Sullivan still had his thick, curly brown hair even though most people in their mid-fifties had gone gray.

All watched as Hyder placed the hologram at the center of the table, and the Battle of San Juan Hill started all over again. The hologram came from the very same butterfly, time-probe that had just avoided being destroyed by a Spaniard's bullet during its intelligence-gathering mission, more than one hundred years earlier.

"He's definitely straying," Alexis Shuntly said.

Joseph Sergi agreed, "Definitely. He's been showing little signs for a few months now, but this is the clincher. He seems reluctant to charge up San Juan Hill."

Hyder nodded. "I agree. All in favor of going to the next level raise your hands." All raised their hands and Hyder declared: "Agreed. We have to do a trip. Got to find out what made Roosevelt lose his . . . his . . ."

"Aggressiveness," asserted Maryellen Muldey.

They all looked at Muldey and nodded their heads.

"Yes, his aggressiveness," stated Hyder. He pressed a button on the table, the door opened and a young man entered.

Ted Mehan, a slim dark haired 24 year old was the head of the Hologram/Robotic Group and whenever there was a meeting of the History Watchers one of his group sat outside the door.

Hyder smiled at him. "Ted, we have to send someone back to the 1800 Club in New York City, time frame 2011. Who's handling that period?"

Ted turned the pages in a small notebook, stopped and ran his finger down a list and said, "That'd be Edmund Scott. He is a direct descendant of Bill Scott, the current president of the 1800 Club for that time frame."

Hyder nodded and turned to the people seated at the table. "Bill Scott handled the Lincoln mission," he said, with satisfaction. "He did an outstanding job of delivering the Gettysburg Address when President Lincoln was incapacitated for a short period. He then went on and stopped a takeover of the White House, which our probes completely missed. He took over Mr. Prescott Stevens' place when he retired. As I said, he did an outstanding job. Especially since it was his first time travel mission. He took to it like a duck to water." Hyder looked around the table at the others. They nodded their heads in agreement. "So, a show of hands if we agree that Bill Scott should handle this case."

They all raised their hands.

DATELINE: NOVEMBER 30, 2011 7:00 P.M. PLACE: THE 1800 CLUB, NEW YORK CITY

Bill Scott was reading Jack Finney's book, *Time and Again*. Although he had read it twice before he found the subject of time travel thrilling, especially now. The first two times he had read it, it was pure fiction. But now, it was reality. Bill knew how the author felt when his hero stepped back into an early New York City. He knew because he had done the same thing. Not the same way as Finney's hero did, but by opening the 1800 Club's time travel portal, set up by the History Watcher's Group.

He sat back, put the book down and sipped hot cocoa from his favorite cup, a Donald Duck mug, as he gazed out the window of his midtown New York, townhouse apartment. It was on the top floor of the 1800 Club and the view was spectacular. He gazed at the fire roaring in the huge wood, brick and stone fireplace with the painting of Prescott Stevens over it. Prescott had run the club for twenty-five years while Bill had been a member for only two years when Stevens picked him to be his successor and, he thought, *That was just a few weeks ago!*

He took a sip of his drink, *It's been a wild five weeks,* Bill thought as he took a bite of an Oreo cookie.

One of the club's rules was to keep a record of any trip back, and Bill must have read and reread all previous trips plus his own exploit a dozen times or more. *Boy,* he thought, *Jack Finney would have loved to have had the club at his disposal when he wrote 'Time And Again.'*

He finished his cocoa and as he peered into the large, ornate 1802 mirror over the washbasin to straighten his cravat, the grandfather clock struck seven-thirty. *Almost eight. Got to get ready for dinner,* he thought as he went to his desk and looked at the evening's menu: *'Steak and potatoes with carrots and baby* onions, all smothered in brown gravy.' *Man,* Bill thought, as he patted his stomach. *I'll have to watch it or I'll grow into this job in more ways than one.*

A knock at the door got his attention. He opened it as he put on his dinner jacket. Standing in the doorway was Matt, the right-hand man to his predecessor who Bill now inherited. Matt was helping to break him in.

"Good evening, Matt," Bill said. "Almost time?"

Matt gave a hint of a bow. "Yes, sir. Dinner will be ready at eight o'clock."

"Did you get a head count, Matt?"

"Yes, sir. Twenty-four members this evening."

"Mmmm, should be a nice evening."

"Yes, sir. I'll check on the food."

"Fine. I'll be down in a few minutes."

"Very well, sir." He walked out and Bill closed the door.

Matt walked toward the staircase and stopped in front of a large mirror on the wall. He spotted a slight smudge and using his clean handkerchief wiped it off. He fixed his bowtie and patted back his reddish, gray thinning hair. He looked close at the mirror and seeing a bit more of his whiskers thought, *Time to sharpen my shaving blade.* The mirror was over one hundred years old and it seemed to be slightly warped as it cheated the viewer of an inch or two of their height. Matt felt it gave his five-foot eight-inch height the look of five-foot six-inch person. The mirror also seemed to lighten the color of his brown eyes and round off his rather pointed nose and high cheekbones.

He glanced back at Bill's door before going down the stairs. Matt knew that the new president of the club would need his help and felt it was his job to guide the young man as much as possible. He grinned inwardly, as he almost never showed emotion as was drilled into him when his father was training him. He was proud to be part of a long line of 'House Men', a name created by his great-great grandfather. A House Man did more than just create a menu, dust furniture and such, rather they ran the house. Of course the master believed it was they who ran it, but the Worthingtons knew better. One of the first things they changed was their dress code. Rather than tails, they wore black single-breasted suits with white shirt, stiff collar, black bow tie and shoes. Working with, rather than under President Stephens, Matt took up the job of collecting both men and women's outfits that might be worn when they traveled in time. Having the correct outfits was needed and he was constantly stepping back in time to purchase them. He also took trips back to furnish the club with genuine objects of the mid 1800s including foods not stocked in the present day. When a time traveler was to go on a mission, Matt set up the rail, ship or aircraft reservations along with hotels and other things needed to complete the mission. Taking a last glance at the mirror he mentally patted his flat stomach as he remembered the new president's love of black and white cookies that he would purchase in a Brooklyn doughnut shop in 1956. He took a liking to them as well, but he was adamant to keep his weight under a number he alone had set. One of the ways he kept trim was by practicing *Hapkido*, a martial arts Cane fighting technique he excelled in.

Back in the den, Bill went over to a turn-of-the-century armoire and took out a white handkerchief. Bill deftly placed it in his breast pocket as he looked in a full-length mirror, and noted that the white stood out crisply against the black, three-piece suit he wore. He fixed the dark red cravat at his neck then bent over and gave a fast swipe to the polished, high-buttoned shoes he wore.

A knock at the door at the rear of his den stopped him. Bill stared at the dark mahogany door with its brass handle and lock, his eyebrows raised.

"Prescott?"

He walked quickly toward the time portal. *Can he be visiting from back then?* Bill thought as he grabbed the key that hung from a gold chain around his neck and quickly unlocked the door. He flung it open and saw his contact from the future, his grandson Edmund Scott, smiling at him.

"Grandp . . ."

Bill quickly put a finger to the time traveler's lips before the young man could finish his sentence. "Hush! Don't say it. I'm not even married yet so you can't call me *grand*-anything. Not yet anyhow." They hugged and Bill said, "Come in, Edmund, come in."

Scott's future grandson walked slowly into the office. Bill quickly remembered that the air of the twenty-first century was a thick, polluted atmosphere that future people could handle for only short periods of time. He pulled out a chair.

"Sit, Ed, sit down."

The tall, slim man did as he was told. "Whew, Gran . . . err . . . Bill, I mean. I know the air in this period is heavy with pollutants, but a guy forgets until he breathes it again." He shook his head. "So, how are you?"

Bill answered with a smile, "I'm fine. What about you? How are you doing? Can I get you anything to drink?"

Edmund shook his head. "No thanks, Bill. Since we cleaned up our water, your water is like a super-bad case of Montezuma's Revenge."

Bill cringed. "Sorry. So, what brings you here?"

"Remember what I said the last time I was here? About Theodore Roosevelt? It looked as if he was losing the daring edge we all know he had?"

A knock at the other door got both men's attention. Bill got up and stopped Edmund as he started to rise. "Stay seated. It's Matt letting me know dinner is being served." He opened the door, and Matt saw Edmund.

Addressing Bill, Matt said, "Excuse me, sir, I see you have company. Shall I have another place set?"

Bill looked at Edmund questioningly.

"Not for me," Edmund said. "Actually, I'll be on my way in a few minutes."

Bill turned to Matt. "I'll be a little late, Matt. Have dinner started, and I'll catch up."

"Very well, sir," Matt said calmly and closed the door behind him.

"You're welcome to join us, Edmund. I'm sure you'll fit in, and none would be the wiser."

"I'm . . . I'm having a hard time breathing and I'd probably pass out in the middle of dinner," the younger man said. He looked at Bill and asked, "Will you have to try and explain to Matt how I entered this room without ringing the front doorbell?"

Bill shook his head. "No. Matt knows all about the club's time travel capability. In fact, he has been going back in time for years and bringing back staples that have been gone from the grocery stores for a long time."

Edmund nodded as he wiped the sweat from his forehead.

"Edmund, maybe the next time we meet, I'll come up to your time. I've never been there."

"I can arrange that. But you do realize it'll be like you breathing the rarefied air on a high mountain."

"I'll try anything once. Now, what about Roosevelt?"

"Well, we had indications of things starting to go differently than they were supposed too. Little things, but changes nonetheless."

"Can you elaborate? I'm fascinated by how you guys in the future can see these so-called 'little things.'"

"Well, you know he had a house on Sagamore Hill in New York. The house was said to be full of animals he had hunted and stuffed. Well, the house has no trophies according to the latest probe we sent back. Not that I'm for him hunting wild animals, but it was the way history went, and we have to find out what made him change." Edmund took a slow breath. "I'm sure you're familiar with his famous charge up San Juan Hill?"

"Sure. He broke the Spaniards entrenched on it."

"Well, a probe just came back and showed us that he didn't make the charge and a group of U.S. soldiers were captured." The time traveler took a shallow breath before continuing. "The enemy used them as pawns to escape. The U.S. finally won the war, but there were more casualties than there were supposed to be. Many of the casualties didn't go on to do the things they were supposed to do in history. It slowed down the progress of the nation to the point that the Japanese became the number one Pacific power and dictated trade agreements for years."

"You got that all from a drone?"

Edmund smiled. "Yes, and our computer projections. It's ironic. Because we did such a good job cleaning up the environment, we can't put a man back there and must use mechanical probes." As if to emphasize this statement he took another shallow breath.

"Because of horse waste and poor sewerage, the air was much worse in the 1800s than it is in your time. It's so bad that we must send drones back. Well, the drawback with drones is that they can't ask questions. They just can't get that one-on-one that a person can get. We really don't know what influenced Roosevelt to change his assertive nature."

Bill nodded, "So, you want me to go back and find the problem and fix it?"

"That's pretty much it, Bill. I can't stress enough how important this mission is. Not just for my time period, but yours, too. The ripple effect will reach your time before mine, and the projections we are getting from our computers aren't good for us at all. We might lose the First World War unless the problem is fixed."

"I have to change history?

"No Bill, not change it, put it right. You've read the history books. Roosevelt charged up San Juan Hill and became vice president, setting himself up for the presidency." The young time traveler closed his eyes for a moment and inhaled slowly before he went on. "Since we first started sending back probes, we've discovered that there's a possibility that events can change unless we help. I mean, we know how it's supposed to turn out, so when we see it deviating, we have to step in and help straighten it out."

Bill said, "Hence, the 1800 Club."

"Right," Edmund responded with open hands. "Your members are students of that time period, as you are. You were an easy choice to go back and help Lincoln's Gettysburg Address when it wasn't happening. Plus, when the club's president decided to retire, you became the logical choice to replace him."

Bill pressed his visitor. "How much time do I have?"

"As soon as you can. It just has to be done right. As you know, we can't let Roosevelt get wind of the fact that you're from his future. There's a chance he'd start doubting himself, thinking that all he achieved was credited to us. He'd lose his self-confidence."

"I understand," Bill, said with a nod, "Prescott explained it to me before he retired. Coax them, but let them take the lead."

"As long as the lead brings them to where history says they went."

Edmond got up unsteadily. Bill took his arm and asked, "Okay?"

The young man from the future smiled weakly. "Just a little woozy. It's hard for me to get used to this time period. If you need anything from us, do you know how to get in touch?"

Bill nodded, as he opened the door. "Yes, I press 'CALL' on the Time Frequency Modulator." Or if I'm in the field, use the text communicator. Prescott said you guys are pretty quick to respond."

"We always have someone assigned to watch for a call or text message. It's pretty important to all of us. I know you understand."

"Yep, I do. After dinner, I'm going to do some research on Roosevelt, identify the main crossroads of his life and try to find the change point."

The two men shook hands. Then, as Edmund started out the door toward the future, Bill called to him. "Hey, give your grandfather a hug, kid."

Edmund smiled, and they hugged.

At dinner, once again back in the 'club time' of the 1860s, Bill took a bite of his steak and thought *dinner is outstanding. I've got to compliment the chef.* He looked around the table. The club members were seated, eating and talking in low tones, mostly of the newspaper headline stating that some rebel troops had raided a U.S. military arsenal and made off with all the munitions.

Among this evening's guests were the Border brothers who sat next to each other and were dressed in period evening clothes. Next to them was Thomas Cradel, a New York stockbroker. He said that he had made his money in the sheep and beef that he sold to the Union Army. Bill knew it was his great-great-grandfather who really made the money and that Cradel was acknowledging him by portraying him in the club.

At the other end of the long table was Colonel Charles Fedders. He was dressed in a U.S. Army, blue dress uniform with crossed-cannons on his lapel, designating him as an artillery officer. He was talking to Emma Walters who sat next to him. She looked exquisite in a long, red dress with opera-length white gloves and her blonde hair upswept in the fashion of the day. She sat with her hands clasped as she spoke to him.

"Colonel, if, as you say, the Union artillery is superior to the rebels, why don't we just always make sure we have an overwhelming number of guns each time we meet them on the battlefield?"

The Colonel smiled, as he dabbed at a bit of gravy on his graying beard. "Ma'am, if it were that simple, the war would be over by now, with us the victors. We must have transportation and men to run the trains. We must have our Navy making sure the Rebs don't sneak ashore and wreck our ports of embarkation. Our great factories must also make belt buckles as well as bullets and bayonets. All this takes away from producing field pieces. But, as I've said in my letters to Mr. Lincoln, he would win in a short time if we followed my plan for producing twice the number of cannons we are producing at the moment."

"Surely you jest, Colonel. You wrote to the President? Pray tell, what was his reply to your great plan?"

"Well, I haven't really heard, yet. He must be very busy with the war and all. Or perhaps he feels he should say nothing while he acts on my plan." He leaned towards her, "Spies you know, Miss Walters, they can be anywhere."

"Of course, Colonel: spies. We must be diligent," she said with a smile.

Bill mentally congratulated her on the way she had handled a rather boastful Army brass hat . . .even if it was his great-great grandfather he was imitating.

After dinner, the guests followed Bill to a large room furnished with overstuffed chairs and couches of the period with a roaring fireplace as its centerpiece. Chandeliers hung from the ceiling and their candlelight's reflected off the well-polished wood floor. Matt served cigars and brandy as small groups gathered and engaged in their favorite pastime: conversing as though they were back in the 1800s.

Henry Osgood sidled up to Bill as he watched the members mingle. "Great dinner, sir. Why, I bet your kitchen staff labored for hours to prepare it."

Bill nodded as he blew a large smoke-ring toward the high ceiling. "Indeed they did, Mr. Osgood, indeed they did." He looked at his glowing cigar. "And a fitting way to end the evening, don't you think?"

"Cuban?" Osgood asked, as he looked at his own glowing cigar.

Bill answered, "Yes. I had a batch brought in just this week. Lucky. The very next ship was stopped and boarded by a

Confederate gunboat crew. Their ship and cargo were confiscated. It's all in the timing, Osgood. Being in the right place at the right time, or in their case, the wrong place at the wrong time. Makes this cigar even more enjoyable does it not?"

Osgood nodded in agreement as he took another brandy from the tray Matt offered.

Bill noticed Emma Walters as she sat with her drink at one of the tables, reading the newspaper. "Excuse me, Mr. Osgood," he said, "I feel I must mingle."

"But of course, sir, please do your duty," Osgood said heartily.

Bill walked through the small crowd and stood over her. "How are you this evening, Miss Walters?"

She looked up and smiled. "Fine, President Scott. And yourself?"

"The same. May I ask what article intrigues you so much?"

She laughed. "I could say it was the latest fashions from Europe, sir, but, in fact, it is the timetable of the trains leaving New Jersey."

"Leaving for where, pray tell?"

"California. That's where the future is, I do believe. San Francisco to be exact."

"Gold fever, Miss Walters?"

Her steel-gray eyes flashed as she answered with a smile, "Adventure, President Scott, adventure! I'd love to take a train as far west as I can, then finish by coach. Maybe see some wild horses. New York is too tame, I feel."

"I'm sure the cowboys out that way would have their hands full with you, Miss Walters."

"Indeed they would, President Scott. You should see the real me."

Bill cringed inside. *She's going to slip up and speak out of 'club time,'* he thought.

She put the paper down and stood, "I'm a quick-draw champion, President Scott."

Bill put out his cigar as he looked at her. "Do you mean that you do fast sketches for a newspaper or other periodical, Miss Walters?"

She smiled at him, as her eyes flashed again. "No sir. I mean a quick-draw champion. A person that can outdraw another in the act of taking a six-gun out of the holster and pulling the trigger before the other person can."

Bill's eyes widened as he reminded himself to read up on all the members' hobbies. "That is amazing, Miss Walters. I have never met a quick-draw champion. How did you come to develop that interest?"

"My father taught me, sir. He had a Colt pistol and became quite good at drawing it. I wanted to be just like him, so I started to practice with it and after a while, I was faster than he was. He was so proud that he entered me in tournaments. Soon we were on the circuit competing with cowboys and want-to-be cowboys, and I was beating them all."

"I'd truly love to see you perform, Miss Walters."

"Perhaps someday you will, President Scott." The clock chimed ten thirty and she looked at it. "I must be off, sir. It's been a long day."

"Will you be back soon?" Bill asked her. "The club is closed tomorrow for some painting, but on the following evening, the menu is fresh trout."

She smiled. "Well, fresh trout! Then I simply must be here."

"Good. Good then. Maybe you'll show me your quick-draw?"

"That sounds fair. Fresh trout for a quick-draw exhibition."

Bill took her hand and did a small bow, "Until then," he said.

She smiled, "Good night, President Scott."

She walked out as many heads turned to watch her leave.

Later that night, she sat in her living room cleaning a six-shot, Colt 1844 revolver by the light of the television. She smiled at a funny line by the TV host. *He is tall, just like President Scott,* she thought. She looked at the pistol, which really didn't need cleaning, but she realized she wanted it to be in the best shape possible to show President Scott. She put the pistol in a red, felt-lined case next to its twin and closed and locked it. *Got to get some sleep,* she thought. *Dad always said, 'never handle a weapon when you're tired.'* She shut the TV off, and the room went dark.

Early the next morning, Bill sat at his computer munching on toast spread with peanut butter and sipping the coffee Matt had delivered. A biography of Theodore Roosevelt was on the screen and Bill was carefully entering notes into a book he kept on his desk.

He learned that Theodore Roosevelt became Governor of New York State in 1899 and often worked in City Hall in downtown New York City. The following year he became President McKinley's Vice President and assumed the Presidency after McKinley was assassinated in September 1901.

Roosevelt had lots of friends including the cowboy, Bat Masterson, whom he named U.S. Deputy Marshal of New York City. A little-known fact was that Roosevelt and Masterson often discussed military strategy, which, some say, aided him in the Spanish-American War.

Intrigued, Bill thought, *Well, I think I'm going to visit Governor Roosevelt. It'll be nice to stroll in New York in June of 1899.* He patted his stomach, *besides I need the exercise.*

He finished his breakfast and went to his dressing room. The time traveler selected a typical outfit of the 1890s: a tan, three-piece suit, a white shirt with a stiff collar and matching cravat with an inexpensive stickpin. Knowing that he planned to do some walking, he put on a pair of soft leather, high-buttoned shoes and topped it all off with a brown derby and walking stick. The new president of the 1800 Club looked at himself in the full-length mirror of his dressing room. "Enjoy your walk, Mr. Scott," he said to himself.

He picked up a period writing tablet and two pencils and put them in a small leather folding case. *Quite dapper for a periodical writer,* he thought. He walked over to an intercom and pressed the button.

Immediately, Matt's voice answered, "Yes, sir?"

Bill folded some writing paper as he said, "Matt, I have to make a trip out the private door."

"I understand sir. Can I be of any assistance?"

"Yes, can you bring me one hundred U.S. dollars, for an 1899 trip? Tens, singles and some coins should do it."

"Yes, sir, straightaway."

Bill put the small leather carrying case in his inside breast pocket and patted it flat. He went to his desk drawer and took out a brown leather billfold with matching identification folder. It held a grainy black and white photograph of himself dressed in period clothes and identified him as William Scott, freelance writer. A tap at the door brought Bill to his feet. "C'mon in, Matt."

Matt entered, carrying a white envelope. He emptied the contents on Bill's desk and said, "One hundred dollars in U.S. currency of the 1890s, sir. Will you be gone long?"

Bill scooped up the bills and put them in the billfold and the change in his pants pocket. "I don't think so, Matt. It's in 1899 in New York City, so it's just a matter of exiting the garden and going downtown to City Hall. According to the old newspapers, Theodore Roosevelt will be working out of there for two weeks, and I'm going to try to have a chat with him. I'll be back by tonight."

"Very well, sir. As you know, the club is closed this evening and you'll be dining alone," Matt pointed out.

"Good. If I'm late, no one will miss me."

"Have a safe trip, sir."

"Thanks, Matt, see you later."

With Matt gone and the door locked, Bill took the key from around his neck and opened the large mahogany door at the back of his den. He took the Time Frequency Modulator from his inside breast pocket and used the keypad to type in his security code: 'President' and added June 6, 1899, 10:00 A.M.

Bill opened the door and walked down the cool, brick-enclosed stairway. At the bottom, he pressed the TFM's 'Activate' button and unlocked and opened the heavy, steel security door.

DATELINE: JUNE 6, 1899 10:00 A.M. PLACE: THE 1800 CLUB'S GARDEN, NEW YORK CITY

He stepped out into a sunny morning in 1899 and heard the clop of horses' hooves on the cobblestones.

Bill locked the door behind him and walked through the lush garden surrounded by eight-foot-high stonewalls, toward the wrought iron gate. He stopped near the small goldfish pond and picked up a tin can of fish food and sprinkled some into the pond.

He took out a cigar and lit it as he peered out into the quiet world of the New York of 1899.

A woman pushed a baby carriage and held the hand of a little boy who wanted to pet a horse pulling a wagon full of vegetables. She scolded him as they approached Bill's gate.

He tipped his hat and smiled. "Good day, ma'am."

She smiled back and looked embarrassed at the boy, who was determined to pet the horse. "George! Stop pulling this instant.

You'll be trampled by that horse and wagon if you don't stop." She looked at Bill again. "Lord, the children of today. I don't know how this generation is going to take our place. All they want to do is play."

Bill nodded and smiled in agreement. "Oh, I suspect they'll do just fine."

He watched them as they went down the tree-lined street. *What a great time to be alive,* Bill thought, as he puffed on his cigar, *Quiet, easygoing times.* He took a deep breath but wrinkled his nose immediately as he got a whiff of horse waste. *Oh well, one must take the good with the bad,* he thought.

He set off in a leisurely stroll toward New York's City Hall and Theodore Roosevelt. Along the way, he bought an apple from a street vendor for two cents and a soda pop for a penny. *A guy could live real well here,* he thought taking a bite of the juicy fruit.

Bill had been back to the 1800s at least a dozen times, yet he never really got over the feeling that people were staring at him. He had to keep reminding himself that he was one of them even though he was from their future. They were living and breathing just as he was. They were not the poor-quality, black and white, grainy photos that he had seen in history books; they were live people with hopes and plans for their own futures.

I have to snap out of this! I need to enjoy the present, or the past as it may be, and get on with the mission, he thought, as he sipped his soda pop.

Bill walked further down Broadway than he had to, just to see the low buildings that would be replaced with one of the most beautiful buildings of its time, the AT&T building at 195 Broadway. He recalled working there for a short time in 1998.

An elderly woman stood on the corner, wiping bird droppings from her wide-brimmed hat. Bill looked up and noticed the wires were still above ground and a favorite perch for thousands of city birds. He also noticed that people tried to avoid walking under the wires whenever they could. He spotted a trolley car with the destination sign on the front stating its final stop was City Hall. *Maybe I'll take it back uptown for the return trip,* he thought.

His walk took him to City Hall Park where he saw a pristine building in the middle of the small, lush park. Although low compared with the rising buildings of New York City, it looked majestic in the center of the green area. He entered the park stepping on the octagon-shaped pavement stones, which led to City Hall. As he went up the granite steps of the building, he was surprised there was only one policeman pulling guard duty.

This is one of the reasons I'm drawn to this era, he thought, *the easygoing atmosphere it has.* The policeman eyed him and tipped his hat. Bill smiled and stopped.

"Good morning, officer, beautiful day, isn't it?"

"'Tis indeed, 'tis indeed. And what might your business be, sir?"

Bill removed his hat and ran his fingers through his thick brown hair. "I'm hoping that I might get an interview with Governor Roosevelt."

The affable policeman answered, "Not my job to say so, sir. 'Tis Mr. Sean O'Hara you'd have to be asking. Mister Roosevelt's assistant, whose office is up the stairs, first door on the right."

"Thank you, officer," Bill responded. "Do you happen to know if the Governor is in today?"

"Aye, that he is. A very prompt man. Always at his desk by eight o'clock, any day he's in town." The policeman smiled and pointed to a group of boys running across the lawn. "Got to do me duty, sir."

The policeman headed off toward the boys, and Bill took in New York's City Hall, the nerve center of the great city. As the time traveler entered the building he noted that the workers were mostly men, all walking at a leisurely pace and carrying paperwork. The doors and windows were all open to the fresh air and sunlight.

No air-conditioning yet, he thought . . . *This is for real, not a picture in some schoolbook.*

At the top of the marble stairs was the office of Sean O'Hara, Assistant to the Governor of New York, as it stated on the door's glass window.

Bill knocked just as a heavyset man in glasses opened the door to leave the room. It was Roosevelt. Bill looked at the future president and was momentarily speechless.

Roosevelt smiled and said, "Come in, come in. I'm just leaving." He turned and spoke over his shoulder, "Sean, you have a visitor." He turned back to Bill and gestured with his teacup, "He'll be out in a minute. He's making his morning tea."

Roosevelt started to walk past, as Bill held out his hand. "Governor, I've always admired your work."

The Governor stopped and accepted his handshake. "Well, thank you, sir. Any friend of Sean's is a friend of mine."

A voice came from the open door, "Actually, your honor, I don't even know this man."

Still shaking Bill's hand, Roosevelt looked him in the eyes. "Well, sir, what would your business be then?"

"I'm sorry, Governor, if I led you to believe I'm a friend of Mr. O'Hara's. In fact, I was told to knock on his door to see if I could possibly get an interview with you."

"That's impossible," said the thin man from behind his boss, "the Governor has appointments all day. Besides, there is a waiting list that you . . . "

Roosevelt interrupted. "Oh Sean. He's here already. And if Mister . . . ?" he raised his eyebrows in question.

"Scott," Bill filled in, "Bill Scott, New York freelance journalist."

"Ah, a fellow New Yorker. Well, Mr. Scott, as I was going to say, if you can keep it to under one-half hour, we'll talk over my morning tea. Good with you?"

"Great with me," Bill responded, unable to believe his good fortune.

O'Hara had a dark look on his face and Roosevelt said, laughing, "Sean, look at it this way, I just did part of your job. And now you can sit and relax knowing where I'll be for the next thirty minutes."

"Governor," O'Hara sputtered, "we have protocol to follow."

"Well," Roosevelt said in a stage whisper, "I won't tell if you don't." He slapped his assistant on the shoulder, which almost spilled his cup of tea. "Come with me, Mr. Scott," and the Governor stepped away briskly.

Bill followed as they went down the hall to the corner office. Roosevelt held the door open, and they entered a bright room with open windows and blowing curtains. A painting of wild animals hung on the wall behind a large desk covered with papers kept in place by paper weights. Next to the painting was a photo of Roosevelt in full military regalia surrounded by a group of men also in military dress.

Bill pointed to the photo and exclaimed, "The Rough Riders!"

"Yes, the Rough Riders. A bully bunch! A very bully bunch! Why, they would have followed me anywhere. A very bully bunch indeed."

"Do you stay in touch with them, sir?"

"A few, just a few. Busy times these, are they not? Why, everyone wants something these days." He spread his hands as he went on. "Unrest on the waterfront, unrest with the immigrants, unrest with first this group, then that group. Positively time-consuming! No, I should like to stay in closer touch with my Rough Riders, but we are all so damned busy these days."

He sat heavily behind the large wooden desk and motioned for Bill to sit in the guest chair facing it. Roosevelt looked back over his shoulder at the photo. "Taken just before we embarked for the war. As I said, 'a bully bunch.'" He raised his teacup to the photo and said in a low voice, "Many are gone now, Mr. Scott, as I'm sure you know. In a way, they were heady days, carefree! In another way, it was a deadly business we were setting out to do."

He paused and took a sip of tea. He looked far away. "Only one year ago, but we were children then, only saw the romantic side. You know, get a medal and tell your story to all who will listen. One becomes quickly aware of one's vulnerability when a bullet strikes the man next to you. Snuffs out a close friend's life like that!" he said as he snapped his fingers. He took another sip of tea and looked at Bill over the cup.

"I am aware, Mr. Scott, of the newspapers these days, stating that I should have thrown caution to the winds and charged up that damned San Juan Hill."

Bill replied, "Sir, I'm not here to question you on your past actions. I was hoping to hear your views on the future of the United States and the world."

Roosevelt pushed back in his chair and clasped his hands over his sizable midriff. He looked at Bill, eyebrows pinched in thought. "Not here to question my war record? That's different, sir. Damned different. You are the first reporter to ask of my views of the future. Well, man, ask away." He sat forward.

Bill had his notepad and pencil ready. "Do you have any plans to run for the presidency?"

Roosevelt answered emphatically, "None what-so-ever, Mr. Scott. None what-so-ever."

Bill was taken aback. "You mean if you were drafted to become president you would turn it down?"

"Yes, I believe I would."

"But isn't that what every politician dreams about? Becoming the President of the United States of America?"

"Mr. Scott, you sound like Mr. O'Hara, my assistant. Why, there isn't a day that goes by that he doesn't ask that very same question."

"I guess I just assumed that you would want to be . . ."

"President? Yes, I know that any man in my seat would use it as a springboard to that great office, but, sir, I cannot."

Bill put his pencil down. "Your honor, if you answer my questions on this matter, I'll keep it off the record. You have my word as a gentleman."

Roosevelt looked at him, "Mr. Scott, I've never heard that said before: 'Off the record.' I like the sound of it. Perhaps . . ."

The door opened, and O'Hara put his head in. "Your honor, we have to meet with the dock leaders and must go over their demands before the meeting."

"They may have to wait a bit, Sean. Mr. Scott and I see things eye-to-eye and need about fifteen minutes."

O'Hara shook his head and slowly closed the door.

"So, Mr. Scott, 'Off the record,' correct?"

"My word, Mr. Roosevelt."

The big man pulled his chair closer and clasped his hands before him on the desk.

"Mr. Scott, I was raised to quickly calculate the probability of success for any decision I made and to choose only those options that would be to my advantage. If there was a chance of failure, it was instilled in me to use a different approach. I used this reasoning when I was in industry and as a commander on the battlefields of Cuba. As far as I know, it has never failed me, or my men. Later, however, armchair generals speculated that I should have charged up that damn hill in Cuba. These 'generals' say that had I made that charge and succeeded, the world would be a much better place. I say to these gentlemen of the press who were not there, I agree with them! If I had made that charge and succeeded, Captain Lewis and his men would have been spared captivity. However, Sir, I go on record as saying the Spaniards might have chewed my men up before we would have made any difference in that battle. No, what I did was ingrained in me since childhood and what every fiber in my body told me to do, 'Stay the course!'" He sat back in his seat and closed his eyes for a second before continuing.

"There was no artillery to cover my troops. And my choice was the only one I could have made. And now, I am being chastised for it. Now, I am being told that it is my fault that another country is the dominant traders in world goods. It's supposed to be my fault that they are the sea power of the Pacific. And with the Europeans at each other's throats, another power is going to stay as the force to be reckoned with, for years to come."

He paused and looked out the window. "Now you see why, Mr. Scott, I cannot become the president of this great country. I would always be making a decision on the side of the safest and easiest thing to do. No, I'm afraid the country needs a strong, determined man who takes chances when it is called for. And, Mr. Scott, I am not that man. I've read the great works of the crusades and knights of old, even cowboys. These are the people the country need, not the present-day Governor of New York."

"You mention cowboys, your honor. What did Mr. Bat Masterson say of your ambitions?"

Roosevelt raised his eyebrows, "Mr. who?"

"Mr. Bat Masterson. The cowboy who is making a name for himself out West. Surely you have heard of him?"

The Governor shook his head. "Never heard of him. I do read the penny papers of the Western adventures of Wild Bill Hickok, Annie Oakley and others but not this Masterson fellow."

Bill shook his head, "Excuse me, sir, for lingering on this. I thought Bat Masterson was a close friend of yours?"

"Sorry, Mr. Scott. I've never heard of him."

A rap on the door and it opened as a determined O'Hara put his head in. "Chief, they need you now."

Roosevelt nodded to his assistant and stood up. He put out a large hand and Bill shook it. "Mr. Scott, it was a pleasure meeting you. I'm sorry if I beat around the bush on things, but now we are pressed for time."

"Mr. Roosevelt, the pleasure was all mine, believe me."

They walked out the door, and Roosevelt disappeared into a crowd of dock leaders.

Bill walked back toward the building that housed The 1800 Club in 2011. He was puzzled. *The books I read on Roosevelt said he was not only a close friend of Bat Masterson's,* he thought, *but also that they used to sit around talking military strategy. I just don't understand it. From all I've read about Masterson, he was a man full of confidence and it rubbed off on his friends, so maybe by not meeting him, Roosevelt simply followed his upbringing and took the safest routes in life.*

He stopped and headed toward a large wooden newspaper stand. *This stand is already looking old,* thought Bill, as he fished for change. He looked over the available periodicals. The old man who evidently owned the stand leaned out and watched him as he thumbed through the *Police Gazette* and a few others.

"What'cha looking for, mister?" the man asked.

Bill looked up, "Um . . . I'm not sure. Do you carry Wild West stories?"

"Another cowboy admirer," the man mumbled, as he reached over his head to an inside section. He passed three magazines to Bill. "Here. I got 'ta keep 'em inside 'cause these kids read 'em without paying. I got'a make a living, too, I tell 'em. But do they care? No. They just want to know what's going on 'cross the continent. They can all go and stay there if ya' ask me."

Bill nodded in agreement to keep him talking. "Do any of these have Bat Masterson stories in them?"

The old man took off his knitted cap and scratched his head. "Bat Masterson, 'ya say? Don't know if I heard of him. Is he a new one? They seem to get new cowboys every time I turn around. Is he a white hat or bad guy in a dark hat?

"Ah, I believe he wears a white hat," Bill said, as he thumbed through one of the pulp magazines. "I hear he's a lawman."

"Well, he better be quick on the draw out there, 'cause if'n he ain't, he ain't gonna be in them books too often."

Bill nodded again. "How much for the three?

"Gimme twelve cents and we'll call it even."

Bill paid for the magazines, rolled them up and put them in his pocket as he headed uptown and home.

Back in the garden he once again took out his TFM and after entering his security code, 'President' added December 1, 2011, 6:00 P.M. and pressed the 'Activate' button.

DATELINE: DECEMBER 1, 2011, 6:00 P.M. PLACE: THE 1800 CLUB, NEW YORK CITY

Bill ate a tuna and tomato sandwich and sipped a large frothy glass of Brooklyn's own, 'Manhattan Special' for dinner that evening as he read the stories in the magazines he had purchased that day, or rather, that day over one hundred years ago. He pushed back his plate and stared out the window at the New York of today. The magazine he had purchased spoke of Annie Oakley and her shooting abilities, Wild Bill Hickok and Jesse James, but not a word about Bat Masterson.

Bill pondered: *Could this be the reason that Roosevelt was a changed man? Masterson was a big influence on him even before he went to Cuba . What if they didn't hit it off? What if they never met?* Bill lit a cigar and paced the floor. Matt came in and removed the dishes. He saw that Bill was in a quiet mood and left him to his thoughts.

According to the Roosevelt he spoke with, the Governor never met the lawman. Bill flopped down on a large, comfortable 1848 couch. He flicked his ash into an upright ashtray and came to a decision. *I have to meet Bat Masterson. And I have to go soon because this is getting eerie.* He booted up his computer and typed into the search engine: ***Bat Masterson: Timeline.***

He scrolled down the cowboy's timeline. Bill found that Masterson was in Dodge City, Kansas, in 1875 and was recruited by Wyatt Earp as his deputy marshal.

He called Matt. "I'm making another trip tomorrow, Matt, and I'll need two hundred U.S. dollars, from the 1875 period."

Matt asked, "Will you be gone long, sir? The club will be open tomorrow."

"Not sure. It'll run without me for a day or two."

"Very well, sir."

"Oh, and another thing, Matt. I'll make out a list of clothes I'll need, along with a Colt pistol and holster. And I'll need about thirty rounds with it. I'll be leaving early tomorrow morning."

"Very well, sir."

The next morning Bill tried on a dark outfit with scuffed boots that Matt had provided from the club's large and ever evolving clothing section. His clothes were well worn and his pistol and holster looked used, as well. He studied his image in the full-length mirror as Matt held a long, black range-coat and a ten-gallon, black, cowboy hat.

"Sir, did the fellows on the wrong side of the law really wear black hats?" Matt queried.

"No, Matt. That's stuff that the pulp magazines printed for the cities on the East Coast."

Matt handed him the 1875 bills and the coat, which Bill put on. He then placed the money in his billfold and satisfied, changed back to his three-piece brown suit and packed his western outfit in a light carpetbag, carrying case.

"Have a safe trip, sir." Matt said, as he watched Bill open the door to the past.

"Will do, Matt. See you soon." He went down the stairs and at the bottom entered into his TFM, 'President' followed by June 10, 1875, 9:00 A.M. and pressed the 'Activate' button and opened the security door.

*DATELINE: JUNE 10, 1875 9:00 A.M. PLACE: THE 1800
CLUB'S GARDEN, NEW YORK CITY*

Bill stood by the garden gate until a horse-drawn cab strolled
into view, and he hailed it.

A big mustached man wearing a frayed top hat looked down
from his high seat and asked "Where to, sir?"

Knowing there were many ferrys crossing to the Jersey shore,
Bill asked, "I need to catch a train to Kansas. What would be the
best way to go?"

The driver scratched his chin as he said; "I'll take you to the
ferry to New Jersey. From there, you can catch a coach and sleeper
to as far west as the weather or them buffalo let ya go."

"That's all I can ask for," quipped Bill as he placed his bag into
the cab's interior, stepped on the iron rung and into the well-worn
cab.

It was a thirty-minute, bumpy ride on the cobblestone streets
and Bill was all-eyes as he passed places he had seen only in the
1800 Club's library. He was happy when the cab pulled over to the
curb as the horsehair-stuffed seat had been flattened by many
passengers before him, making it feel as though he had sat on a
wooden board the entire ride.

The ferry ride was an adventure itself with bucking horses and
drivers trying to calm them down as they all jockeyed for the best

position . . . it reminded him of the chariot race in the movie, 'Ben-Hur.' The ship rode low in the water, its single tall stack belching thick, black smoke, and Bill thought the other steamers came a little too close at times. He marveled at the sight of the much lower New York City skyline but was glad when the trip across the Hudson River was over.

Bill remembered that the train depot was attached to the Ferry Terminal and soon was at the station in front of the ticket counter.

A very efficient man behind a small window sold him a ticket that stated in small type: ***"The holder of this ticket may ride all the way to Kansas on this railroad company line, and if they must change for another line, because of weather or Buffalos, this line will honor the seat or the sleeping quarters he has paid for."***

The ticket agent said the price for the entire trip was seven dollars and the train was being fired up, so Bill could board immediately on Track 2.

The time traveler carried his gear out to the train and couldn't help but stand in front of the large engine, as he looked wide-eyed at what he thought to be an oversized Lionel train set. *My gosh,* he thought, *I feel like a kid on his birthday. This is for real!*

The train belched steam and groaned as the boilers waited to send power to the big steel wheels. He watched as a man dressed in coveralls, oiled the gear that connected the wheels. The engineer actually wiped the condensation that formed on the sides of the engine. *What pride these men have for their train,* he thought as he watched them perform their maintenance on their version of the family automobile. Bill was brought back to reality by the call, 'all aboard.' He ran down the wooden platform and stepped up onto a short steel staircase that brought him into the car.

The conductor checked his pocket watch and waved to the engineer as he stood with one hand on the steel handrail. The train started with a sudden lurch followed by a smoother acceleration as the man swung up and onto the step.

Bill entered the car and was immediately surprised by the dark interior. The walls were painted a dark brown and tan and the windows were too dirty to allow direct sunlight. *Not the crew's fault,* thought Bill as he got a closer look at the windows, *the soot from the engine has permanently darkened them.* Because of the fear of lit embers entering the cars, all the windows were closed. The seats were overstuffed, yet hard, and businessmen puffing cigars filled most of them. In a very short time, the entire car was a smokehouse.

It had been a long day, and the smoke-filled car helped Bill decide it was time to turn in. He asked the trainman to show him his sleeper and was thankful the sleeping car was two back from the smoker. He removed his shoes and hung them on a peg on the small berth's wall, then lay down with his clothes on. Bill pulled the curtains closed and even though the bed was as hard as the seats, went right into a deep sleep lulled by the clickty-clack of the wheels on the rails.

The rocking motion that put him to sleep also woke him the next morning. The engine purred and the steel wheels clacked on the rails as the springs rocked the cars like a boat on the high seas.

The time traveler went into the small washroom that was at the end of each car and was glad he had decided to bring a few items from his time, such as toothpaste and a toothbrush. The overhead, gravity-feed system provided only a slow, warm trickle of water. The toilet was a smooth wooden seat with an open hole in the bottom that allowed you to see the passing railroad ties fly by, and if you opened the small window to freshen the air, smoke and sparks flew in. *Still,* he thought, *I am back in the 1800s. It's what I always wanted, and here I am.* He straightened his clothes as best as he could in the tiny compartment and smiled to himself. *Start every day as though it were the first day of the rest of your life.* He unlatched the door and stepped out onto the tight aisle and walked forward to the dining car.

Low wooden partitions surrounded tables that sported white linen tablecloths. Most were taken already, and Bill was surprised at the girth of most of the men. He thought, *the people of my time are always crying that we are the fat generation. Well, this proves the contrary. Then again, these people don't have the benefit of knowing about fats and cholesterol, and indulge as they see fit.*

A burly man finished his breakfast and Bill slid into the seat he vacated. Even after noticing the girths of his fellow passengers, he was lured by the smell of fresh bacon, sausage, and eggs with toast smothered in butter. He ate every bit of the breakfast that was set before him and washed it down with two cups of coffee from the smiling waiter.

Making sure that there was nobody waiting for a seat, Bill then followed the others by lighting up a cigar. *Oh well, when in Rome,* he thought as he listened to the various conversations in the car.

The talk was mostly about past trips taken by his fellow riders. So far, the consensus was that this was a good trip. No bison ripping up the track while trying to scratch the itch caused by their new horns, no miles of wild horses crossing in front of them, and no Indians. *At least not yet,* Bill thought as he settled down to watching the Wild West roll by.

Later that day, at the end of a small town called, *Rattlesnake Haven,* the train stopped to take on water. The conductor announced that it would take almost an hour to fill the engine's water tank so most of the passengers got off to stretch their legs. Bill went into town and was surprised to see that the hot sun kept most of the townsfolk off the streets. Horses stood with their heads hanging low, all tied to rails in front of stores, their tail whipping back and forth chasing flies. One of the places with the most horses out front was the bar, *"The Dustoff,"* and Bill decided to step in out of the sun.

He stepped through typical, swinging doors and went to a long, wooden bar. It was cooler inside but not by much. Bill thought, *well, at least it's out of the direct sunlight.* Not wanting to seem nosey he stood at the bar and used one of the three large mirrors behind it to look around. Most of the round tables were full of card players and many had silver nuggets in front of them. There was an upright piano against the wall and a skinny man with a thin mustache played some songs unknown to the time traveler.

A tall, heavyset man with his black hair parted down the middle asked as he wiped down the bar, "What's yer drink, friend?"

Bill looked at what two men down the bar from him were drinking and said, "Beer."

The bartender pumped a long wooden pump-handle attached to a keg beneath the bar and it splashed beer into the large, chipped glass he held beneath the spout. Seemingly satisfied that the foamy head was larger than the yellowish beer, he placed it in front of Bill and said, "Four cents or a pinch of silver."

"Afraid you're going to have to settle for the coins, my friend," said Bill with a grin as he put the coins down. He remembered that the bartenders and other tradesmen in the boomtowns were picked because of the size of their thumbs and index fingers. The reason was simple: if a miner paid in gold dust or silver nuggets, the man with the larger digits was able to get a bigger 'pinch' from the bag the miner carried it in.

He took a pull of his beer as the barman walked to another customer. *Hey*, he thought, *pretty darn good!* He saw a sign behind the bar with chalk printing that stated: ***Pork sandwiches 7 cents or 2 pinches of silver. Ham/boiled or fried-same price. Steak when available-15 cents or 6 pinches of silver. Potatoes or carrots extra.***

Bill decided to stay with the proven foods of the railroad and not take a chance with a town that will probably disappear as soon as the silver does. He finished his drink and left to stroll down the main street. Once again it was deserted except for a group of dogs sniffing around. A sharp blast of the train's whistle told all to get back aboard and Bill walked back down the tracks to the huffing train. He got back as the engineer was shifting the waterspout from the filler cap on top of the train's engine back to the large, wooden water tank.

Boy, he thought watching something that never takes place anymore in his time, *this is the best! I have to start bringing a small camera along on these trips.*

Hopping aboard he got to his seat as the train blew its whistle once again and started to roll along. It was a constant battle between the people who wanted to open the windows to fight off the heat and the people with window seats who were burned by the hot sparks as they were sucked into the car.

Relief came after five days when Bill heard the conductor announce that Dodge City, Kansas, was about an hour away. Although it was a fantastic experience, the time traveler was happy to take leave of the train. He reminded himself to bring more underwear next time he took a cross-country trip in this time period. And if possible, another suit, a lightweight one, plus extra socks. *Lessons learned,* he thought as the hot train slowed to a stop.

Alighting from the train, he saw a one-horse buck board wagon which passed for a horse-drawn cab. Even though the town was in walking distance he knew it was a chance to get some information, so he waved to the driver, a young boy with long, black greasy hair tucked under a yellowish straw hat that was frayed all around the brim. The shoeless boy jumped down and grabbed Bill's carrying case. He was evidently happy to be hired.

"Welcome to Dodge City, mister. Where to?"

"Not sure. Is there a hotel around here?"

"Yessir, the Splinter House," answered the talkative boy, happy to have gotten a fare, "It's not really called the Splinter House, it's the Coronado, but it's made o' wood and it's old and if'n ya' walk on the front walk without yer boots, ya' get a splinter."

Bill smiled. "I'll make sure not to take my boots off then."

"Want to go there, mister?"

"If you recommend it, why not?"

The boy beamed at being listened to. Bill took the seat next to him. The youngster pumped the reins and shouted, "Giddyap!

Bill held on tight to the wooden seat as the buggy hit a few ruts and asked, "Tell me, son, do they serve food at the Splinter House?"

"Yessir, but if'n you want good grub, go to Pearl's on Main Street. She's a real good cook. And she washes the dishes after every meal. I know 'cause I work there." He said proudly, "My name's Timmy."

"Then Pearl's it is, Timmy," said Bill, as he looked at sights seen only in his dreams. He noticed that the boy kept his wagon's wheels in two ruts that ran down the right hand side of the street and any wagon coming toward them drove in the two ruts on their side. *Pretty smart,* he thought, *ride the groove and have fewer bumps on the wheels. Of course, they probably all disappear after a rainstorm. Then again it doesn't rain too often here.*

Timmy took him to the Coronado Hotel on the main street.

"How much, Timmy?" the time traveler asked as they pulled up in front of the hotel.

The boy removed his hat and held it in his hands as he said with a shrug, "I dunno, mister. Nobody ever rides with me. They mostly jus' walk ta town."

"Well, then," said Bill as he dug into his pocket, "how's about ten cents?"

Timmy's eyes bulged as he stammered, "Ah-I mean, well, sure mister. Ten cents is sure okay with me. Are ya sure though?"

"I'm positive."

"Thanks a whole lot, mister an' if ya need help getting' around town, jus' find me in Pearls." He tipped his hat, slapped the reins gently and rode off with a big smile on his freckled face.

Bill smiled to himself as he stepped over a dried mud hole and piles of horse droppings to reach the front walkway. *Timmy was right,* he thought as it creaked beneath his feet, *it's old and worn.*

The creaking alerted the clerk as Bill approached the small front desk. The short, chubby man with thick, red sideburns jumped to attention, as Bill dropped his traveling bag on the floor, raising a small dust cloud.

"Yes sir! Welcome to the Coronado. How long ya' figure on staying?"

"Not sure, a day or two."

The clerk turned a dirty book toward him and pushed a straight pen and inkbottle forward. "Put yer marker here or just plain put an 'X' if'n ya' need to."

Bill printed, "Bill Scott."

The clerk turned the book around again. "Mr. Scott. That'll be one dollar a night.

Bill counted out three singles and laid them on the counter. The man immediately put the cash in a drawer and said, "Another fifty cents if'n you want a towel and one dollar for hot water for a bath. We serve breakfast and dinner, but it's not part of the dollar. Ya' gotta' pay extra for that."

Bill put down another half dollar. "A clean towel and I assume there's cold water available?"

The man grabbed the coins and stuffed them in his pocket rather than the drawer, as he looked around. He handed Bill a long ornate key and said, "Room 203, and I'll bring yer water up myself."

Bill climbed the creaking stairs to the second floor, opened the door to Room 203 and entered. It was a dusty room with one window that was dirty except for a circle in the center where the last person tried to wipe away the grime to see out. The window had a poor excuse for a curtain and the walls were covered with wallpaper that sported a flowered print. The furniture consisted of a small wooden table and chair, a single bed, a small washstand with a washbasin and a dented, tin pitcher sitting in it. On the table stood the only light source: a candleholder with half a candle in it.

He put his bag on the bed, looked at his pocket watch and realized how hungry he was at only five-thirty in the afternoon. *I better get some food before it gets too dark to find my way around town, and,* he thought as he glanced at the small candle, *I think it's going to be a dark evening.*

A shuffling outside his door announced the clerk with his water. Bill opened the door and saw that the pitcher was half empty from spillage and the towel was damp from the same spilled water. He took the pitcher before the clerk spilled more, poured the contents into the pitcher in the room and gave him back the empty one.

"Can you tell me which way to Pearls?"

"Step out of the hotel, go right and cross two streets. It's on the corner. Say, did I mention we serve food?" the desk clerk asked eagerly.

"Thanks, I have to meet someone there," Bill, responded.

"Oh? Who might that be? I mean, yer new in town, after all."

"Just an old buddy." Bill shrugged his shoulders casually to end the conversation with the nosey clerk and closed the door.

He washed as well as he could with the small amount of water provided. Leaving his hat and cravat behind, he stepped out to get dinner. Not sure why, but maybe to just be in vogue, he strapped on his pistol and holster, but he let his jacket cover them.

The evening was warm with a slight breeze once again bringing the smell of horses his way. As he walked in the direction of Pearls, he heard a clanging and came to the blacksmith shop. Bill had to force himself to keep walking past the big man working iron on his anvil. He wanted to stop and watch, but he realized he'd be the only one looking, as it was a common sight for the people of this era.

He walked past the marshal's office and saw a tall, slim man with a droopy mustache, sitting on his desktop cleaning a shotgun. Their eyes met, and Bill got a chill. He kept walking but looked back once and saw that the man followed him with his eyes.

Looking out of place, with crisp, clean linen curtains on the windows, was Pearls. Even if he did miss the 'PEARL'S FOOD' printed on the window, he couldn't miss the aroma of Pearl's kitchen. The time traveler looked through the window and saw that the room was about half full. Bill entered and stood by the door as he might in his time, then quickly realized there was no Maitre D' to seat you, it was seat yourself.

The man from the future took a corner table so he could look out the window and observe all around him.

A white haired, heavyset woman came over and smiled. "Hello, mister. If you're hungry, we have two pork chops, fried onions, sliced boiled potatoes and corn. Corn bread'll be ready just about the same time yer about to have coffee. Now, if you just want a small meal, I have a cold, sliced pig's foot on hard, brown bread. I can pour some hot gravy over it if'n ya like. The dinner'll cost you one dollar, and the other will cost you twenty cents. What'll it be, stranger?"

"I'd like to try your pork chops, ma'am."

"Ten minutes," she said with a smile, "and believe me it's worth the wait. I killed the porker myself jus' this afternoon."

Bill smiled and picked up a newspaper from the empty table next to his.

The Dodge City Journal was a local paper and, it stated, 'Proud of its circulation of three hundred and sixty-five.' However one of the customers drew a line through the number three-hundred and sixty-five and printed 364.

The paper's large headlines screamed, *"WYATT EARP TAKES GRAFT"* and led into the article that continued, *"says Aaron Eddilson, who as you know would be the next marshal if he had his way. When asked for proof, Eddilson stated, 'Proof? The proof is that he (Earp) has friends all over town asking citizens to vote for him in the upcoming elections. His friends just happen to own the largest stores and companies in Dodge. It is simple arithmetic. They pay him to watch their businesses, and in return he gets the people to vote for him. I, on the other hand, have no one to back me in these elections, and I go on record as saying I do not receive any monies from these groups.' When asked by this newspaper of his past experiences as a peace officer, Eddilson said he had none, but a person had to start somewhere and he has great ideas for Dodge. When asked to expand on these ideas for our fair city, Mr. Eddilson accused the paper of being one of Earp's financial backers who would turn these ideas over to Mr. Earp to use for his own benefit. (Ed. Note. This newspaper has never taken nor given favors for any position in the great city of Dodge.)*

"It's not true, you know."

The deep voice startled Bill, and he quickly lowered the newspaper. Facing him was the man from the marshal's office. He was dressed in a faded black, three-piece suit with a black wide-brimmed hat. His white shirt was sweat-stained around the collar and he wore a black string tie. A long dark mustache framed a strong, square chin. He motioned to the paper. "As I said, stranger, it's not true."

Bill nodded as he put the paper back on the table. "As you said, I'm a stranger in these parts, and I don't know the facts, so I take your word for it, sir."

The man looked at him with steel blue eyes and said nothing.

Bill returned his gaze and asked, "Did you follow me or are you here for food?"

The man pushed back his hat and relaxed a bit. "Now, why would I want to follow you? You walked past my office and looked in. Then you looked back. That's just not done unless a person wants to catch a fellow off guard. You are clean-faced, not the average cowpoke. You have a nice shiny pistol and a handmade holster, not the average store-bought. You walk with a confidence of a man who's done things. You stepped over and around horse dung with the grace of a man used to dodging opponents in fisticuffs or military combat, yet you are a bit young to have been in the War Between the States. As to whether I followed you here, well, this is the best place in Dodge to eat. Does that answer your question, Mister. . . ?"

Bill rose halfway out of his chair, put out his hand and said, "Scott, Bill Scott." The man slowly extended his hand and each tested the other's grip. Bill continued, "I'm a freelance writer. I came out here from New York City to write about Dodge City. Not the dime novel trash they sell in the cities, but the real story. I did my time with the military, as you said, and I have spent some time in a fighting ring. And I assume that you are Marshal Wyatt Earp?"

"I am. And, as I said, this is the best place in Dodge to eat."

Bill smiled and sat as he shook his head. "Got to hand it to you, Marshal, you noticed an awful lot about me in a short time."

Earp nodded. "Keeps a man alive, Mr. Scott."

"Guess it does. I once heard a general say that the winner of the battle is the person who can ward off the battle by knowing his opponent and how he would react to any given move. You, I believe, are that type of person, Marshal."

"Sir, you honor me." Earp bowed slightly from the waist. "Will you join me in the tavern for a drink after dinner, Mr. Scott?"

Bill nodded. "I will, and it's Bill."

"Good, Bill. Call me Wyatt."

"Well, Wyatt will you do me the honor of joining me in dinner?"

"On one condition, Bill. Allow me to sit in your seat as I truly get an itch if I think someone could easily come up behind me without me knowing."

Bill stood as he offered the chair with its back to the wall, "Please be my guest."

They sat and Bill noticed that Earp kept an eye on whoever entered the eatery.

Bill and the marshal skipped coffee and left Pearl's as Wyatt explained the town's customs and problems. He said he wanted to outlaw guns in Dodge. But in order to do so, he said he needed a few good men to help him enforce the law. He said with certainty, "More than one cowboy will test it, and has to be stopped short."

As they approached the Long Branch bar, Bill saw an interior lit by oil lamps and candles. He felt as if he were in an old-time cowboy movie. There was a piano player, saloon girls and card games going on in the garishly painted, smoke-filled room.

The roar went down a notch or two as Wyatt opened the swinging doors. They walked over to the bar. The bartender whispered something to Earp and motioned to a middle-aged, heavy-set man who had grabbed a chorus girl by the throat. The marshal turned to Bill and made a space for him at the bar. "Have what you want and I'll have a Red Leaf Whiskey," he said.

Bill ordered the same as the lawman walked slowly over to the troublemaker. Earp put a hand on the man's shoulder and the troublemaker spun around and drew a knife. The crowd of people around them suddenly parted. The man's eyes opened wide as he recognized Earp. He dropped the knife and put his hands up. Bill noticed that Earp's gun was still holstered.

The marshal pointed to the door and commanded, "Out." The man ran out into the night, bringing the crowd to a roar of laughter. Bill made room for Earp at the bar. They picked up their drinks, and Bill clicked Earp's glass, saying. "Cheers!"

Earp looked quizzically at Bill and said, "Good health!" They downed their drinks as the noise level in the room went back up and a happy bartender poured them another round.

At two in the morning, the place was as full as ever. Bill was starting to feel the Red Leaf, but it didn't seem to bother the marshal at all. Earp ordered another two as he looked at Bill questioningly.

Bill caught the glance and asked, "What?"

Earp looked at him with raised eyebrows, "What, what?"

Bill answered, "What is it you want to ask me?"

"What makes you so sure I want to ask you something?" the marshal countered.

"Just seems like you did. Seems like you want to ask me something but are holding back."

"And I shouldn't?"

Bill said, "No, you shouldn't. Never hold back."

Earp paused, and then said, "I'm looking for a few good men for my office. Would you like to be one of them?"

Taken off guard, Bill blurted out, "Me? Heck no, I'm no lawman."

The marshal continued, "You're better than most. I've been watching you. You keep your back to the bar or are watching your back in the mirror. No, you have what it takes. Just got to see how you handle that fancy gun of yours."

Bill hoped to end this turn of the conversation by saying, "I'm a writer, and a good writer is constantly aware of his surroundings. That's all."

"Naw, there's more to you than you show," Earp said quietly. "But if that's your calling, so be it, partner."

Bill hurriedly tried to move on to a new topic. "Speaking of a few good men. I heard a name," he said as he took out a small notebook and read, "Bat Masterson."

"Bat Masterson? You mean William Masterson?"

Bill was about to say something when he remembered that Bat was a nickname. His real name was William Barclay Masterson. "Yes, William Masterson. Isn't he a reliable man?"

Enthusiastically, Earp said, "The best! Absolutely the best! But as a lawman, never! Tough man, but there has never been a worse shot in Dodge. I'd be looking for a replacement in a day or two, and I'd have lost a good friend. Besides the newspaper editor would have my head. He's their best writer."

The crowd's attention suddenly turned to a man outside the tavern screaming Earp's name. They looked at the marshal; they wanted to see some action before going home.

Earp shook his head and asked the bartender, "What time is it, Clem?"

The bartender took out his timepiece. "Three o'clock, Wyatt."

"Damn, I thought I'd have one night where I didn't have to kill some fool. Guess not." He gulped down the two drinks and ordered another.

Bill turned to him and asked, "Is there anything I can do, Wyatt?"

"No thanks, Bill. Stay aside. This is what I get paid for. Wonder where Mr. Eddilson is about now?"

He walked to the swinging doors with his drink in his hand. Outside, the same big man he had thrown out earlier, stood with a large knife in his hand.

"C'mon out, Earp, c'mon out, so I can cut you good."

The marshal walked slowly out the door, stopped and downed his drink. He turned to a chorus girl, gave her the empty glass and took her long, white scarf. He wiped his mouth with it as he walked toward the man.

"Listen, mister, I don't want a fight. It's after three in the morning, and I've been drinking all night. What say we sleep it off?"

"No! You're yellow, Earp!" The big man shouted. "I'm gonna cut you up real bad. And I ain't waiting 'til tomorrow neither."

Wyatt wiped his mouth again as he got closer to the man. He stopped just out of reach of the man's knife-hand and spread out his arms, the white scarf dangling from his left hand.

"Mister, I'm just not up to fighting anyone right now, so why don't you go . . ." He dropped the white scarf, and for a split second the knife-wielding man's eyes inadvertently glanced at the dropping fabric. Wyatt caught the man's jaw with a right cross and he dropped like a stone. The lawman took the knife, tucked it in his boot, and turned to Bill. "Guess we should call it a night, eh, Bill?"

Bill nodded. "Damn, that was a classic, Wyatt."

"Just proves the hand's quicker than the eye. He'll wake up tomorrow and if he still wants some of me, he'll end up in Boot Hill. Most likely, he'll be out of town by the rooster's call." He tipped back his hat and said, "Had a good evening, Bill. See you tomorrow?"

"Yes, and I did too." Bill responded. "Good night, Wyatt."

Bill slept very well on his first night in Dodge.

The next morning the pocket watch Bill brought along from the future chimed softly and woke him. His head hurt from a hangover but not as bad as he thought it would. He popped two aspirins he had also brought along, then washed and shaved with the water left over from the night before.

He changed into his western outfit and went out. On the way to Pearls, he walked past the marshal's office. It was locked and a small sign read: ON PATROL." Bill wondered if he was really on patrol or just sleeping late.

Breakfast was as good as any Bill had had in any century. *Got to watch this eating,* he reminded himself feeling the tightness of his belt.

At the counter, Pearl wiped her hands on a clean apron. "How was it?"

"Outstanding. Ever think of going to New York City and opening a place there?"

Pearl put a hand on her hip, "Now, why would I want to do that?"

"So I could eat there every day," he said, "and not have to travel hundreds of miles for a great meal."

She laughed. "Instead, I'll give you a copy of my cookbook."

"Fair enough," said Bill opening his billfold, "Can you tell me how to get to the *Journal's* office?"

"Sure, honey. Just go out and make a right. Walk three streets, and it's on the corner. Can't miss it, it's the only red brick building in town."

After thanking her and leaving a generous tip, Bill stepped outside. *Another cloudless day,* he thought fixing his hat brim to block the rays of the early morning sun as he strolled down the creaking wooden sidewalk. When he reached the first corner, the marshal came around it and they nearly collided. He was cradling a double-barreled shotgun.

"Morning, Marshal," Bill said.

"Morning, Bill," Earp responded. "Sleep well?"

"Like a log, and you?"

"Same. Nice duds. You sort'a lost that dude look. Now all ya need is some upper lip hair."

"I really needed to air out my other clothes and I look terrible with a mustache."

Earp grinned, "Don't remember if you said how long you'd be in town?"

Bill shrugged. "Not sure. I'm going to try to get an interview with B . . . Mr. Masterson."

"Masterson is at his desk right now. Just saw him typing away. See you later. If ya hanker for lunch, you'll catch me at Pearls' at noon."

"Lunch it is marshal." They both nodded and continued on their way.

Bill arrived at the *Dodge City Journal*, scraped his boots on the front step and opened the door. There were about a dozen wooden desks with piles of paper stacked on top of them, along with early model, Royal typewriters. Two were occupied, and Bill recognized Masterson from his archived photo as he pecked away on his typewriter.

Not a tall man, he stood at five-feet eight inches and tended to be on the portly side. He had long, black hair parted down the middle and a small mustache, as did most men in this time period. Masterson wore a white shirt open at the collar and wide black suspenders held up his black pants.

Bill approached him, and Masterson looked up. He squinted at Bill, then stood and offered his hand. "Mr. Scott. Am I right, sir?"

"Yes, you are." Bill smiled as they shook hands. "Are you that good a reporter that you know someone's name by looking at them, sir?"

"Ha. No sir, not at all. I just had my morning coffee with the marshal. He told me of last night's adventures in Dodge, and he made mention of your name. More than once I might add."

"Nothing bad I hope."

"Nope! All to the good. He spoke of you wanting to write about the real Dodge, not the Dodge they turn out for the eastern trolley riders."

Bill nodded. "That's what I'd like to do. And I'd like nothing better than to have your collaboration on it."

"My collaboration? Why mine?" Masterson asked with surprise. He turned and pointed to an older man working at another typewriter. "Why not Chester? He's been living here for thirty-four years. I've been here for just one year."

"Mr. Masterson, I've read your stories. They strike a style unlike others I've read. I'd really be proud to have you join me in this venture."

"And where would this be printed, Mr. Scott?"

"I do not yet have a publisher, Mr. Masterson, but I'm sure of the mission I'm on. And would you address me as Bill?"

"Well, if we are to work together, Bill, then please call me Will. Now," he pulled a chair over for Bill, "sit and tell me your storyline." He sat back, his arms crossed behind his head.

Bill faced him across the desk. "Will, I want to write about the difference between the average man of the West who can shoot well, and the man who can't. I don't need to write about the cowboy, that's been done many times over. I mean the average man who has to make a living in the West of today."

"Bill, any man can shoot a gun. Is this the story you really want to pursue?"

Bill shook his head. "No. Any man can pull the trigger, Will. But not every man can shoot well. That's the story I want to do. I want to know if the better shot has more confidence in himself, more charisma, more gumption, more admirers, pretty much more everything, than the man who just doesn't have it."

Masterson had the look of a man deep in thought. "This does sound different from any dime novel I've read. It's like looking into many a man's soul. It'll be like telling them, you can either stay here in the West, or be on your way. It's going to be a rude awakening for many. It's like the Roman Empire making gladiators. All can swing a sword, but just a few rose to the top and fame."

"Right, Will, its true journalism. No sugarcoating the cowboy with his six-shooter. He may be one in ten, twenty or fifty."

"Okay, Bill. I'll work with you on this. What do you want me to do?"

"There's a second part to this, Will. I'd like to take an average man with poor shooting ability, teach him to shoot well, and then write about how his life changes. I'd like you to pick this man."

Masterson pulled his chair closer to Bill's. "Pheww! That's a tough one. That'd be like fingering a man who's not up to snuff, so to speak. It's sort of insulting him, telling him that we know he's not as good as his neighbor." He got up and walked to the coffee pot sitting on a potbelly stove. "Want some coffee? It's just warm, got a low flame on, so we don't melt the place."

Bill joined him and took a mug from the rack. Masterson poured two cups and swished the rest in the pot. "Chester, want the last cup? Still warm."

The elderly, gray haired man got up and walked slowly to the two men. He looked at Bill, pulled on his long, gray mustache and said with a smile, "Will's a wily guy. He knows whoever finishes the last cup has to make a new pot."

Masterson smiled. "You're in luck this mornin', Chester. I feel the need for some real coffee today, not the kind you make. I'll be making a fresh pot."

"Damn civil of you, Will, damn civil," he said as he poured the last cup. Chester walked back to his desk and spoke over his shoulder, "To a real reporter, the story is everything, Will. Remember that. To get the story is the thrill. To nail down what no one else has, that's the thing. The gentleman has a good idea. He needs an average gun handler and came to you." He sat at his desk and looked at both men over his coffee mug. "I'd be the average gunslinger, but I'm over the hill. What this story needs is an average man with gumption. A man who would back up his thoughts even if he can't shoot worth a lick. Will, I hate to say it, but you're that man. I saw you take that big stick we keep to fix the print jams and whack a man on the head 'cause he cussed in front of some women folk. Didn't bother you that he wore a six-gun. You'd be perfect for this story. Might even get ya' a job in some big city paper."

Masterson shook his head, "Sorry, Chester, I'm the worst shot for miles around."

Here we go, thought Bill as he addressed Masterson, "This could be the answer, Will. If you are as bad a shot as you say, you'll be perfect. And look at all the pluses. We don't have to insult a towns person. Nobody would have to know you were taking lessons. And you'd get to be a better shot, too. You're in a win-win situation. What do you say?"

Will smiled. "A win-win situation? That's a good one. Never heard it said that way before. Would it be you giving me lessons?"

"No, not me, uh . . . my cousin," he said with crossed fingers, "I'll be back in town in about two weeks and then we can start. Okay with you?"

"Just so we have it straight, no one is going to know about this, right?"

"Right. Just us. That's a promise."

Chester cleared his throat. "Boy, does this ever mean the end of me making fresh pots o' coffee. Hallelujah!"

Bill and Masterson smiled.

DATELINE: DECEMBER 9, 2011 PLACE: THE 1800 CLUB, NEW YORK CITY

Although he was gone for over two weeks, when he returned he entered December 9, 2011 into his Time Frequency Modulator.

Man, I love time travel, he thought, *but as the saying goes 'there's no place like home.'* As he removed his boots, Matt set down a pot of coffee and the peanut butter and jelly sandwich that Bill had asked for as soon as he arrived.

"Pleasant trip, sir?"

"Very. I think I found the source of the deviation in the time stream. Has Miss Emma Walters been in attendance during my absence?"

"She was here the evening before last."

"Was it a large gathering?"

"Sixteen members, sir. Tonight's list shows thirty-seven reservations. As you know sir, a Friday brings in most of the members."

"Matt, I'm going to take a long hot shower and go to bed until 6 P.M. I intend to be in attendance tonight."

Matt nodded and left with Bill's Western clothes. His face showed that he was aware of their aroma.

At the dinner that evening, Bill sat at the head of the banquet table. He had on a light gray, three-piece suit with a dark blue cravat at the neck of his starched white shirt. He wore white spats with his highly polished, black button-up shoes and had a dark blue silk handkerchief in his breast pocket. He felt refreshed and sharp. The diners were seated at the long table.

The day's newspaper headlines shouted about the poor workmanship of the Union's rifles. The table conversation was mostly about the lathes being used by the Northern factories versus the European types.

Jerome Thompson, who had money in a large firearms factory in New Jersey, claimed that the Europeans were paying large sums to spread rumors of their products being superior to the North's. Nathan Hersey denied this loudly in his Cockney accent.

All is fine in The 1800 Club, thought Bill.

Seated at the middle of the table was Emma Walters. Bill nodded as he caught her eye. She returned his nod with a smile.

After dinner, Bill broke away from a group of members discussing cotton prices and its production, which they thought would be key to the rebuilding of the South after the war.

Seeing Emma Walters alone on the balcony, Bill grabbed two brandy snifters and made his way toward her.

"Beautiful evening isn't it, Miss Walters," he said as he offered her the brandy glass.

Taking it, she smiled. "Yes, it is. Have you been away on business, President Scott?" They touched glasses.

"Yes, I have. And I'll be going on another trip soon." Bill liked the way the moon highlighted her blonde hair. "On our last conversation, Miss Walters, you promised me a demonstration of your gun handling. Does that invitation still stand?"

"It does. When would like to see a demonstration, President Scott?"

"Tomorrow is Saturday. Are you available on such short notice?"

"I'll make an exception for you, sir. Here at the club?"

"That would be perfect. What time is good for you? If it's around eight pm, I'll have dinner set for us."

"Eight it is sir."

A group of people came out onto the balcony and joined them. This time the conversation revolved around the hot-air ballooning going on in France. Bill noticed that Emma slipped away before the last person left.

The next evening, at eight o'clock sharp, Bill's intercom buzzed. He reached over and punched the button. "Yes, Matt?"

"Miss Emma Walters to see you, sir."

"Thanks, Matt. Please bring her up."

Two minutes later there was a tap at his door. Bill opened it and saw Matt with Emma. "Good evening, Miss Walters," Bill said. "So nice of you to join me for dinner."

"Nice of you to invite me, President Scott," Emma replied.

Matt closed the door and left them alone in the den. Bill noticed that she was dressed in close-fitting cowhide pants and jacket while he was dressed in period clothing. She had a traveling bag with her. He went to a small bar by the window. "Drink?" he asked.

She put the bag down by the bar, "Yes, a white wine, please."

He poured a white and red wine and handed her the white. He raised his and said, "To a good evening."

They touched glasses and she nodded. "Yes, to a good evening."

Each took a sip, and Bill looked at the bag she had brought. "Your equipment?"

She nodded. "Yes, two Colt 1844 revolvers and their belt and holsters."

"The making of an interesting evening, Miss Walters."

Bill guided her to her seat at the small dinner setting. The table was located in his favorite spot: a bay three-window alcove that, depending which window you looked out of allowed a view of New York City down to the Statue of Liberty and beyond, across the Hudson River to New Jersey and all of upper New York City. The fine-linen covered table was set for two, with china, cut glass and silverware from the mid-1800s, with a tall candle set in a silver candleholder in the center.

Emma exclaimed, "President Scott, this is overwhelming! The table and chairs, the settings, all from the 1800s, am I correct?"

Bill nodded, "Yes, the table and chairs are 1863, and the settings and cutlery are 1864. Do you approve?"

"Yes, I do. Very much, sir."

"Miss Walters, may I call you Emma?"

She answered with a nod, "Yes, you may."

"In that case, I'm Bill. Please be seated."

Matt entered and served them crab bisque soup. The dinner consisted of trout, small potatoes and green beans with a white sauce.

They finished and Emma smiled. "Trout, potatoes, green beans. Wow, all my favorites. Did you just guess?" she asked.

"I try never to have to guess, Emma. I simply checked your past dinner requests. I hope you like strawberry ice cream for dessert."

"Again, my favorite. You did your research well, Pres. . . . I mean, Bill."

"Not as well as I should have, Emma. I totally missed the entry in your membership application that stated you were a quick-draw champion. I can't wait to see your handguns and Emma, I suggest that we relax the 'No speaking Out Of Club Time' rule this evening."

Her smile showed her agreement.

Matt served the ice cream, and they both had coffee.

Later Bill led Emma to his den where she picked up her travel bag and took out a leather case, gun belt and holster.

"Are you familiar with handguns, Bill?"

"Yes, but not six-shooters."

She nodded and passed him a pistol.

Bill held the Colt, checked that it was empty and spun it around his finger. "I was with the U.S. Navy SEALS for a time, and we had to become familiar with all types of guns. Usually with automatics though, not revolvers. So, I'm familiar with pistols, but not fast draw." He handed her the gun. "So, show me what a fast-draw champ can do."

She automatically flipped open the chamber and checked that the weapon was empty. Next, Emma strapped on her belt and holster, tied the holster to her thigh, put the Colt in it and stepped back.

Bill watched as he noted, *Wow! She's another person now. She's zoning in on the draw.* And just like that the pistol was in her hand and pointing downrange.

Bill blinked. "Wow! That was fast!"

"Thanks. I'm off a bit. Haven't had time to practice for a few days."

"Well, I couldn't tell. Wow, that was fast."

"Thanks again."

"Let me see that one more time."

"Okay," she said, and once again Bill saw just a blur, and the gun was out and pointing at an imaginary target.

"Emma, you are fast! Is there anyone faster?" He asked with admiration.

"Not that I know of."

"Do you teach classes?"

"I taught an old boyfriend once, but you can only teach so much. It's either there or not. You have to have it. Are you looking for lessons?"

"Not me, a friend of mine. Interested?"

She frowned slightly. "Teaching my ex-boyfriend was one thing, but a stranger. I'm not sure."

Wanting to keep the conversation going, Bill asked, "How long do you think it would take for someone to become faster?"

"Become faster? So your friend has had lessons. If someone else tried to teach him, I'd have to break old habits first."

"Then you are saying yes?"

She shrugged her shoulders. "I really don't know. It's not what I do, I mean, the teaching part. That's a different thing entirely. How much training has he had? And is it a he? Men have different learning traits than women."

"It's a he, and he's been around guns his whole life. I believe he just needs a good teacher."

"Who's the prospective student?"

Bill looked at her. "I knew sooner or later I would have to answer that question. I once had an art teacher who used to say, 'a picture is worth a thousand words.' Well, it's true. In order for you to believe the prospective student's identity, I have to completely gain your confidence. I thought of a way to do that, so, let me ask you a question: If you could have anything, within reason, from New York City in the 1800s, what would it be?"

"Anything? That's easy, an Allen Pepperbox double-action revolver."

Bill made a note of that on a pad and went on. "And where and when would you be able to purchase one in New York City in the 1800s?"

Emma crossed her arms, "Easy again. Aberdeene and Withers on Seventeenth Street, off Broadway in 1861. That was the place where many Union Army officers bought their 'boot weapon,' a backup to their regulation rifle and pistol. Sort of a last-ditch weapon. Small but deadly at close range."

"Expensive?" Bill wanted to know.

"Yes. And in great demand now, too."

"And why do . . ."

"Why do I want it? Not for money. My grandfather owned one and had to sell it during the Depression to feed his family. It was a gift from his father who said it saved his life during the Civil War. Grandpa is ninety-two and it'd really make his day to have another just like it. Of course, that's all wishful thinking. There are just a handful left and all are owned by collectors who would never part with them."

Bill looked at his pocket watch. "Will you do me a favor? Stay here and wait for me to return, say, in about ten minutes?"

"You want me to wait here while you go out? I . . . I don't know, I mean, that's sort of . . ."

"Inappropriate. I know, but I need you to trust me on this. Believe me, you won't be disappointed." He looked at the grandfather clock, "Nine twenty-five. About ten minutes is all I ask. Okay?"

Emma was perplexed but smiled. "Well, it is different, but then again the whole idea of this club is different. Fine. I'll wait here."

"Good. There's coffee and if you need anything, just ring and Matt will get it for you. Be right back."

Bill slipped out the door at the rear of his den, rushed down the stairs and at the landing took out his Time Frequency Modulator and entered 'President' followed by December 10, 1861, 4:00 P.M. and pressed the 'Activate' button then opened the security door.

Bill walked briskly through the garden, opened the gate and locked it behind him as a cab came up the street. Bill waved him down.

The driver tipped his hat as Bill got in, "Good day, sir. Where to?"

"How fast can you to get to Aberdeene and Withers on Seventeenth Street and Broadway?"

"It's normally a ten-minute ride, but hold tight sir." He slapped the reins on his horse's rump. "Giddyap."

Bill held onto the leather straps next to the cab's window as it sped down the cobble-stoned streets. *Closest thing to seat belts,* he thought as he was bounced around.

Just under ten minutes later, Bill held a small pistol as he spoke to the clerk in the armament shop. "It's a work of art."

"Yes and a good choice, sir. I've had many a soldier come back and thank me for this saver. As you can see it's a caliber .31 with six barrels and can almost be concealed in the palm of your hand. We do get a lot of calls for this type."

"I'll take it."

"Want to come out back and test fire it?"

"No thanks, I'm sold, and can you sell me about fifty rounds for it?"

"Yes sir." The clerk wrote out a receipt. "Twelve dollars and fourteen cents, sir." He wrapped the revolver in paper, and Bill put it in his pocket.

He was back at the club in a little over thirty minutes. He stuffed a five dollars in the driver's hand, ran through the club's garden then up the stairs. Outside of the door he set the TFM to ten minutes after he left and unlocked the door.

DATELINE: DECEMBER 10, 2011 9:35 PLACE: THE 1800 CLUB, NEW YORK CITY

He entered the room and stood in front of Emma, a little out of breath.

She smiled, "You have a great library."

"Thank you. Now all I need is the time to read them. Thanks for waiting." He handed her a small parcel. She looked uncertain.

"Go ahead, open it."

She removed the wrapping, and her face lit up as her hand told her what she was holding. She slowly removed the pistol, her eyes wide and her mouth open in amazement.

"How . . . how . . . how did you . . . where did you . . . I don't understand?" She gazed at it. "It's an authentic Allen Pepperbox double-action revolver. Manufactured in 1837, according to the patent date stamped on the barrel. My God, it's like new! A six-barrel, .31 calibers with the conventional trigger. This is fantastic!"

She looked at him. "Where did you get it? There's no way you could have known I'd ever ask for this particular gun, and I don't think you have every gun ever made behind that door."

Bill put his hand in his pocket and handed her a fistful of bullets. Once again, she stared. "They're brand new. And I don't mean manufactured today. I mean made in 1837. How is it that they aren't even slightly handled or dented? This is almost impossible."

He then handed her the receipt. She stared again and said in a whisper, "It's dated today's date, but 1861! And the paper is fresh, not yellowed and stiff like old documents. Plus it's on Aberdeene and Withers letterhead. No way you could have forged this so fast. What's the story, Bill?"

"Then you do believe it's authentic?"

"Absolutely. Please tell me where you got it?"

"It's yours."

She shook her head and put the pistol down. "No way! Thanks, but I will buy it from you if it's for sale."

"If I put a price on it, the price would be to give my friend gun-handling lessons."

"Done!"

He looked at her. "Sit down. Let me get you a drink. I've got a story to tell you."

She sat and picked up the gun again. "It's perfect," she whispered as she looked up at Bill getting her a drink. "Who's the person I have to teach?"

He handed her a drink and looked into her eyes as he said, "Bat Masterson."

"Bat Masterson? You mean, like, his great-great-grandson?"

Bill came over and sat next to her. "Emma, the other evening you said you would love to take a train as far west as you could. I said you would be a lot for those cowboys to handle and I meant it."

"I remember. So, is my teaching job in some sort of a cowboy-reality place?"

Bill shook his head, "No, it'll be teaching the real Bat Masterson how to shoot . . . in 1875." He put his hand up to stop her from speaking, "Emma, this club has the ability to travel in time."

She stood and placed her drink down. "Okay, the evening's over. It was fun for . . ."

Bill rose too, and said imploringly, "I can prove it to you. I left here a while ago, went back to New York in 1861 and purchased that revolver. Look at it. As you said, I couldn't have known what you were going to ask for. Yet, I granted your wish."

She shook her head, "But time travel's impossible."

"Is it? Well, I thought so, too, until Prescott Stevens, our past president, showed me. And now, I'm ready to show you. I know you can handle it. You're an adventurer. And it's fun! Believe me."

She looked at Bill and shook her head again. "This is just outrageous . . . "

Bill took the key attached to the chain around his neck from inside his shirt. "Come with me. I'll take you back to 1861 right now. It either happens as I say it will, or it doesn't, as you say it can't. You have nothing to lose."

She shrugged her shoulders, "Fine. Let's go."

Bill picked up a mid-1800s women's cape that was draped across one of the easy chairs and handed it to her. "I suggest you put this cape on to cover your 21st Century clothing in case we pass some people."

Emma tied the string at her neck and the long cape did its job of covering her clothes.

Bill was already dressed in period clothing and he smiled and held out his hand. "Shall we?"

Oh boy, Emma, she thought, *you've heard some lines before but this is the best.* She rolled her eyes at Bill and said, "Okay, let's go."

Bill opened the door, and she studied the hissing gas lamps illuminating the descending stone staircase. They came to the final door at the bottom, and Bill quickly loaded his TFM and pressed the 'Activate' button. He opened the security door and they stepped out into the garden.

DATELINE: JUNE 10, 1861 9:45 P.M. PLACE: THE 1800 CLUB'S GARDEN, NEW YORK CITY

Emma walked out slowly. Her eyes grew wide as she looked around at the flowers and ferns all teeming with life as fireflies flitted about. She stopped and gazed at the small pond with goldfish that shimmered in the light of the gaslight lamp mounted on the wall. Bill watched her as she approached the gate to the street outside the garden. It was a warm evening with a light breeze that made the gaslights seem to be dancing.

Emma said, "It-It's warm! But this is December and yet . . . " She shook her head, "This is impressive. But how do I know that I'm back in 1861?"

Bill opened the gate and stepped out. He pointed to a soft glow on the corner. "Gaslights for one." He pointed to the street, "Cobblestones and horse waste."

She shook her head and recoiled slightly as she smelled the horse waste in the air, "This could all be a kind of reality setting. No, I need real proof."

Bill offered her his arm, and she looked at him, eyebrows raised. "It's how a gentleman and a woman walk about in this time. You know that. For now, just pretend you are in the club. Agree?"

She nodded and took his arm, "Agree. Lead on, sir."

Bill took her to the corner, and she looked up at the gaslight.

"I think I need more proof," she said.

Bill nodded, "Give it a minute or two. Sooner or later a . . . " he stopped and listened, "I think you're going to get your proof soon enough."

Bells clanged and horses' hooves were heard along with steel-rimmed wheels bouncing on the cobblestones. She instinctively held tight to Bill. Suddenly out of the dark burst four horses pulling a red fire engine that belched smoke and steam. A man in a black rubber coat and sporting a thick mustache slapped the reins as another sitting next to him pulled the cord to the bell and the horses quickly turned the corner. Holding onto the rear of the steaming engine were three more men dressed in firemen's clothes of the 1860s.

Bill pulled her back from the street as doors and windows opened and people started coming out to watch the action. Looking down at her open toe shoes Bill said, "You're not really dressed for downtown New York, 1861."

She thought of her close-fitting clothes beneath the cape and the women of New York City with their wide flowing dresses. "Oh my, right you are. I don't fit in here at all."

They quickly went back into the garden. Bill asked, "Want to sit here for a while? It's my private spot." She nodded and they sat on a stone bench in the shadows.

"There are times I come down here just to escape our time, have a good cigar and think."

She fixed her hair and looked up at him. "Was that really a fire engine going on a call in 1861, or am I going crazy?"

Bill smiled, "You're not going crazy. I'll explain all I can to you, but I have to know that you accept the fact that we can time travel."

She shook her head yes. "Oh, I believe it all right. This is amazing, it really is, but, why me? Why do you want me to teach Bat Masterson how to shoot? And if I couldn't shoot, would you have showed me all this?"

Bill shook his head, no. "There'd be no reason to show you. Maybe sometime in the future. That's what the club is all about. And I wouldn't ask you to do this if you weren't a member. But you already are halfway in the past each time you enter the club. Physically and mentally you were in the 1800s when you dress and meet with the other members. Right?"

"You're right." She looked at him and grinned. "When can we go back out there?"

He grinned back and answered, "First let me give you the short story as to why we need Bat Masterson to be a good gun handler. Okay?"

"Go ahead, this I have to hear."

An hour later Bill had told her all about the mission. It started to rain and they went back up to his office and 2011.

DATELINE: DECEMBER 10, 2011 11:15 P.M. PLACE: THE 1800 CLUB, NEW CITY

She wiped rainwater from her shoulders as she came through the door. Matt entered the den with refreshments.

Over coffee, Emma looked deep into the black liquid. "So, in a nutshell, Roosevelt is not the aggressive, confident president we know of from our history books. He didn't charge up San Juan

Hill, and we lost more men than we should have. And because of all this, Japan became the dominant country in world politics, and we take second or third place."

Bill nodded as he put his cup down. "We know that Roosevelt was a huge admirer of Bat Masterson. They used to sit and talk about military tactics. Roosevelt needed a guy like Bat to bounce around ideas. But if Masterson wasn't handy with a gun, he could never have become a lawman, Roosevelt would never get to admire or meet him, and Teddy would lose his guiding star."

"Wow! Bill. That's wild. But let me ask you, does he want gun-handling lessons?"

"This is the sticky part. He thinks I'm a writer looking to do a piece on the pros and cons of being a good gun-handling person."

"You mean gunfighter."

"Well, not really. Masterson is an upright man who can't be pushed around. He's just a terrible shot. I convinced him to take lessons as an aside for the story we are working on together. Whether he's good or not with a gun, he's going to be the same person and in his case, a good person. Believe me, I wouldn't ask you to teach Billy the Kid to shoot. We need Masterson to be good enough to have confidence in himself and let Roosevelt hear of him and meet him so history will take its natural course."

"Where do we start?" Emma asked, eager to begin.

"When you are ready we take a cab to the ferry going to New Jersey. From there, we take a train out to Dodge City, Kansas. I'll go over the clothes and things you'll need for the trip."

Emma pressed him, "When do we start?"

"Tomorrow, if you want. I suggest you get some rest. It's not the easiest trip I ever took."

Emma's eyebrows raised, "I thought time travel could put you . . . well, anywhere you want? Why do we have to travel?" She raised her hand, "Not that I don't want to. I am looking forward to every second of this trip. I want to experience it all."

"I know what you mean. And it's too bad the time unit that sends us into the past can do it only from one place, and that's to and from this building. It's been on this spot for over a hundred years. Next time I speak with the people from the future, I'm going to see if they can hook it up to a GPS unit or something that can place us in any spot we want. But, like you I enjoy having to take the same transportation systems that the people of the time period we visit did. It gives me a feeling of being one of them as we all experience the same trials and tribulations."

The grandfather clock struck midnight and Emma stood up. She held out both hands and grasped Bill's. "This was the most fantastic evening in my life." She looked at the pistol on the table. "What do I owe you for the revolver?"

"No charge. It's a business expense, and I hope your grandfather likes it."

"He will, believe me. Now I have to concoct a story about how I got it."

"Your problem, not mine."

They laughed as Bill walked her to the door. "Tomorrow, Matt will outfit you for the trip."

"I'll see you early in the morning. Good night, Bill, and thank you so very much for a great evening."

DATELINE: JUNE 25, 1875 PLACE: DODGE CITY, KANSAS

One week later, the train conductor let everyone know that Dodge City was thirty minutes away. Bill sat in the dining car as Emma entered. He eyed the men as they watched her walk by them. She wore her blond hair swept up beneath a stylish, wide brimmed, brown hat with a black and white feather protruding from the crown. It matched her wide-shouldered, short brown jacket and long flared skirt. Her high-buttoned shoes made her taller than most of the other passengers and she walked through the bouncing car with grace.

Wow, thought Bill, *even with a minimal amount of makeup on she's a knockout.*

Emma smiled as she sat next to him. "Five o'clock," she said. "Bet it gets dark early around here."

"Wait until you see how dark it gets. You set?" Bill asked.

"Yes, and am I glad you told me to bring my own towel."

Bill looked at her large bag, "I'd love to know what else you have in that travel bag . . . damn, it's heavy!"

She smiled. "Just stuff we women can't be without," she added with an air of mystery, "all very top secret you know."

"Is the pistol I gave you in there?"

She shook her head, no. "No, I gave that to my grandfather before I left. I told him I traded a few of my pistols for it. He was so moved, it was a beautiful moment."

Bill smiled as he felt the train starting to slow down.

Fifteen minutes later they got off the train in Dodge City, and Bill spotted Timmy with the buckboard hoping to get a customer. He waved to him, "Timmy, over here."

Excitedly, Timmy slapped the horse with the reins and brought the wagon over. "Mr. Scott. Glad you came back." He removed his hat, "and this time ya brought yer wife. Wow, she's pretty."

Both Bill and Emma blushed, "Ah, no, she's my cousin, Miss Emma. She's on her way to California and is going to stay here for a few days. Think there's room at the Splinter?"

Timmy replaced his hat and helped Emma with her bags. "Shucks, Mr. Scott," he said, "there's always room at the Splinter. You gonna stay longer this time?"

"Not sure, Timmy."

The young boy slapped the horse on the rump with the reins and took them to town. As Timmy took down Emma's bags, Bill gave him a dollar bill.

"Gosh, thanks, Mister Scott. Like I said, if'n ya need me, jus' call an' I'll be there ta help ya."

At the Splinter the same clerk was at the desk. He licked his palm and slicked back his thinning hair as he explained to Emma that he'd be only too happy to bring hot water to her room for a bath . . . no charge. Bill smiled and said, "Thanks, but I could never let you carry such a heavy burden. When Miss Walters wants to bathe, I'll carry the water up for her." The clerk had a forced smile on his face.

Bill helped Emma up the stairs with her bags, and then brought her some water to wash up.

"Emma," he said, "I suggest we have supper as soon as you are ready. There are just a few street lamps here, and I don't want us to wander off in the dark."

She nodded. "I really want to see as much of Dodge as I can."

He smiled. "As much as you can by the half dozen street lamps. Tomorrow, I'll give you the grand tour."

Pearl's diner was brightly lit and the usual customers were there. Bill looked around for Marshal Earp, but he wasn't around. Pearl shuffled across the room and stood over them, one hand on an ample hip.

"Welcome back. Couldn't stay in New York without Pearl's cooking, could ya?"

"After a meal at Pearls," he said to Emma, "you never venture too far away."

Pearl hit him on the head with her towel. "Aw, go on now. You two hungry or just want a cold snack?"

Emma looked at Bill. "I'm famished. You?"

"Me, too" he answered. "What do you recommend, Pearl?"

"Easy 'cause there's only one choice. Tonight I made roast beef, white whole potatoes, corn on or off the cob, onions and beef gravy. And for gravy-dippin', hot corn bread. Got some goat's milk, too."

Bill looked at Emma. "That's good for me. You?"

Emma smiled and said, "Me too, but hold the goat's milk. Any wine?"

Pearl looked at her, then at Bill "Well, we got a real live one here, don't we?" she said. "Wine it is. Don't ask white or red honey, you get what we got open."

"Good," Emma said.

Pearl walked over to another couple and started her talk all over again.

Emma smiled. "What a happy soul."

Bill winked, "And she can cook, too."

After supper he paid the bill and, as Pearl put the cash in her tin box, he asked, "Is Marshal Earp around?"

The storeowner shook her head. "He's out with a posse chasing some critters who tried to rob our bank."

"Do you know if Masterson went with him?"

"Masterson? The writer? No. I saw him yesterday. He was in for lunch."

Bill said goodnight and stepped outside with Emma. She was looking up at the stars.

"Bill, look how bright they are. No city lights to take away the darkness. Just the way nature meant it to be. This even beats the 1800 Club."

"I know. That's one of the perks about this job. We get to see things as they really were. When I first made a trip back, I was amazed to see everything in color. I was so used to seeing grainy black-and-white photos I started thinking that's the way it was."

Emma was quiet. A tear slid down her cheek. The moonlight glistened on it and caught Bill's eye.

"Hey," he asked in a low tone, "what's wrong?" He wiped the tear away.

She sniffed and kept looking up at the stars. "She's dead. That wonderful woman who just fed us supper and wished us well as we left. She's been dead over one hundred years."

Bill held her. "Hush. She's not dead. She's as alive and warm as us. She's living right now. It's we who are out of place, so to speak. We came back over one hundred years, so are we born yet? No, we're not born for another century. Yet she sees and accepts us as natural as we should accept her. In fact while we are here, she has a whole future in front of her. We came into their world, and they are as alive as we are. Forget that we are from the future and just let your club training take over."

Emma looked at him, then through the window at Pearl as she swept her restaurant floor. She sniffed and patted her nose with a white handkerchief. "You're right. How silly of me."

Bill shook his head. "No, not silly, natural. It shows that you have feelings and a love of history and the past. Not silly at all. In fact, I'm proud that you're a member of the club and I'm glad you decided to make the trip."

"I'm okay now," she said as she wiped some makeup off his jacket. "Thanks for being here."

"No problem. I suggest we get some rest. Tomorrow we start work."

Emma stifled a yawn. "Right you are. Tell me, do you bring me hot water tomorrow morning, and how does one put in a wake-up call?"

"One has to bring an alarm clock and I did in the form of my pocket watch. It has a built-in alarm. I'll set it for seven o'clock, tap on your door, and as you get up, I'll bring you the water, then get mine. Deal?"

"Deal." They walked back to the Splinter and said goodnight. It was a long day and neither missed the train's rocking motion and fell asleep right away.

The next morning, after two trips of carrying warm water to Emma's room and one for himself, Bill was ready for breakfast. He waited in front of the hotel and smoked a cigar.

"A nasty habit."

He turned to see Emma standing in the doorway. She was dressed in a long blue skirt and matching vest which covered a white blouse buttoned up to the high neck. The hem of her dress rested lightly on the top of her low heel black leather shoes. Her hair was pulled back into a French braid and she wore a small flat straw hat with a blue sweatband. Emma also carried a small frilly parasol to ward off the hot sun.

"Do you approve?" she asked as she popped open the small umbrella and swirled around.

He smiled and dusted off his boots as he found himself hoping she approved of his all-black attire. He threw down the cigar and, as he stamped it out said, "I do. I really do. Is that what you had me lugging all the way across the continent?"

"Well, you told me to make sure I had extra clothes," she answered with a grin. "Shall we eat? I'm famished again."

With her hand on his arm, they walked over to Pearls.

An hour later, after a big breakfast of fried ham and eggs topped off with two cups of coffee, they left the restaurant to start their mission. Emma asked, "Bill, I know we have business, but can I stroll for a bit? I'd like to see the real Dodge City."

Bill looked around at the quiet street. "If you feel ready for it, no problem."

"I do," she said excitedly.

"Fine then." He pointed toward the newspaper building. "I'm going to be in that red brick building. It's the *Dodge City Journal* and it's where Bat, I mean, William Masterson works as a writer. In fact, it'll give me a chance to let him know his teacher is a woman." He looked at his pocket watch. "Let's meet back here in about, say, thirty minutes?"

Emma agreed and they walked opposite ways.

In a few minutes Bill entered the building and saw Masterson sitting at his typewriter. He looked up, rose, and they shook hands warmly.

"Bill, how've ya been?"

"Fine, just fine." He looked over at Chester. "Hello, Chester, how's the world treating you?"

The reporter looked over the eyeglasses balanced on the tip of his nose and answered, "Oh dandy, just dandy. I write pearls of wisdom and the danged editor cuts my copy. So, I'm continually in a dandy mood." He took a sip of coffee and held up the half empty mug, "Thank the Lord for inventing coffee."

Masterson asked eagerly, "How was your journey, Bill? I haven't heard of any train breakdowns." He handed Bill a coffee mug full to the brim.

"No problems at all, just a long, hard ride. Have you given our project any thought?"

"Plenty! I'm rarin' to start. Did ya bring your cousin?"

"I did. I'd like to talk to you about that."

Masterson put a cover over his typewriter and turned to Chester. "Chester, I'm going to take the rest of the day off."

"What do you mean, the rest of the day off? It's not even begun yet. What will I tell the boss when he asks why your seat is empty?"

"Tell him I'm on a project and doing some interviews. And, by the way, you can have the rest of the coffee." He smiled as Chester threw a crumpled sheet of paper at him. "See ya tomorrow."

As they left the office, Masterson asked, "So, where is your cousin?"

"Taking in the sights. You know first time in Dodge. Will, I never did ask, do you have a quiet place we can practice undisturbed?"

Masterson squinted in the morning sun. "Quiet and unnoticed. Yeah, I got a little piece of land a mile out of town. I have my horse and wagon behind the office. Where we meetin' yer cousin?"

"We are going to meet in front of Pearls in about ten minutes. Why don't you get your rig and meet us there?"

"Good enough. See ya in a bit."

Meanwhile, Emma walked along the dusty street, taking note of the many things that weren't reported in the history books . . .

mainly, the smell, and the flies! As she walked along the wooden sidewalk, a group of cowboys rode slowly into town. A group of young boys ran after them. She stood transfixed as they went by . . . they were dirty and all need a shave but they were the real thing. She suddenly realized that a dead man was lying across the saddle of one of the horses. Emma was horrified to see a swarm of flies following the group. She felt herself getting sick until she noticed others hardly glancing at them while some of the young boys ran along side of the group. *A normal day in Dodge City,* she thought, *just another day.*

She felt a presence by her side and saw Bill. One of the cowboys tipped his hat to him. Bill nodded in return.

"That's Wyatt Earp."

"The Wyatt Earp?"

"Yes. As I told you, he's looking for a deputy, and it's up to us to get Masterson ready to take that job."

"Well, I'm ready," Emma said.

Bill pointed up the road with his chin and said, "Here's our ride now. And the driver is William Masterson. He's not known as Bat, yet."

"Does he know I'm a woman?"

Bill clenched his teeth and raised his eyebrows. "Well . . . he will in a minute. Don't forget you're my cousin on your way to

California. I don't think he'll want a woman staying around reminding him that she was his teacher."

Driving his rig down the dusty street, Masterson spotted Bill standing there with a woman. *Wonder where his cousin is,* he thought. He stopped and motioned to Bill to climb aboard as the woman looked up at him. *Pretty,* he thought, *don't remember seeing her in town.* He was startled as Bill helped her up and placed her next to him on the wooden seat and then settled down next to her. He looked at Bill questioningly.

Bill said, "William Masterson, this is my cousin Emma Walters."

"Your cousin?" Masterson asked, confused.

Emma put out her hand, "Pleased to meet you, Mr. Masterson."

He felt himself staring. "Ahhh, the pleasure is all mine, Miss Walters."

She turned her blue eyes to him, "Emma. Please call me Emma."

Masterson looked at Bill then back at Emma. "Well, Miss Emma, I'm Will." He looked at Bill once more. "Your cousin? Am I right in saying you are in town with two cousins?"

"Nope. Just one; Emma."

They pulled away from the wooden sidewalk and Masterson looked straight ahead while Emma's head was on a swivel as they left town.

She's a talkative one, thought Masterson after a while. *How hot does it get around here, does it rain much, how hard does the wind blow, is there much sand blown about? Seems ta me that she asks questions that no other women ever seemed ta care about. Least no woman I'd ever met.* He still looked straight ahead as he answered her questions.

Finally, they went over the little bridge that signaled the beginning of his acre of land. On top of the hill was a small log cabin surrounded by oak trees and a low fence. The land around here was fertile and it was a good investment. *Some farmer will want to buy me out,* he thought.

Once by the gate, Masterson jumped down and tied up the horse as Bill helped Emma get down off the wagon. Masterson walked up the cabin's three wooden steps.

"Come on inside. It's cooler in here," he said holding open the heavy wooden door for them. Emma entered and Bill followed, carrying her bag.

Inside the cabin was a small kitchen, a round knitted rug on the floor with a wood burning stove and wooden sink with a water pump. Two cabinets were built into the wall on either side of the sink and Emma saw dishes and mugs with a few pitchers.

Masterson opened a small wooden door and tossed his hat onto a bed. There were stairs going up to the second floor. *Nice and clean,* thought Emma, as Masterson worked the pump handle in the sink. Water poured out, and he caught some in a mug. He offered it to her. *Delicious,* she thought as she drank.

"Come and sit," he said. He escorted them to a small living room with a fireplace centered on the far wall with a rifle above it. Masterson kneeled down and blew on the hot embers and the fire roared to life as he placed a split log on it. The room had a rocking chair and a sofa anchored by another round, knitted rug centered on the floor. In a corner sitting on a small wood desk, was a Royal typewriter and a stack of writing paper. Beneath the desk was a three-legged chair while mounted on the wooden wall above the desk was an oil lamp to illuminate the work area.

Bill and Emma sat on the sofa and both were happy to be off the hard wooden seat of the buckboard.

"Coffee will be ready in ten minutes," Masterson said, as he hung a coffee pot on the iron arm and swung it over the flames. He sat and looked at both of them. "Now, Bill, if you don't have another cousin in town, does that mean that Miss Emma here is going to teach me how to handle a gun?"

Bill nodded, "Yes, Will. Is that okay with you?"

"Not sure. I mean, with all due respect, Miss Emma, you don't come from these parts and it shows. I mean, you're a dainty little thing and . . . well, it just ain't right."

"Isn't right."

"What?"

"Isn't right. The correct way to say it is, 'It isn't right,' not 'ain't right.' As a writer, you should know better, Mr. Masterson."

He sat back at this. *Dang! She is right,* he thought, *and she says it right straight out.* Addressing Emma, he said, "Excuse me, Miss Emma, I just mean the last teacher I had was a little old grumpy woman. That's all."

"I bet she was a good teacher, though. You seem to be a good writer."

He perked up. "Have you – have you read my stories, Miss Emma?

"Yes, I have. And I think the project you and my cousin Bill are working on is going to be well spoken of. And please call me Emma."

Masterson found himself staring at her again. He mentally shook his head as he reached for the coffee pot. "Coffee? Miss . . . I mean Emma."

"Yes, Will, I'd love a cup."

As they relaxed, Bill motioned to the rifle over the fireplace. "Nice rifle. What kind, Will?"

Before he could answer, Emma spoke up. "Kentucky rifle. It first appeared about 1810 and they were mostly plains guns. That's a .45 caliber probably with a 44-inch barrel, a double-set trigger, a low front sight and a fixed open rear. It probably weighs eight or nine pounds and made, I'd say in 1830 or 40."

Both men looked at her with surprise.

"You sure do know your guns, m'am. It was made in 1837. My daddy gave it to me. It'd take out a jackrabbit's tail at one hundred yards."

Bill turned to him. "Did you ever get one at that range, Will?"

"Yep, more than once."

"But I thought you were a terrible shot?"

"I am, with a handgun. But with this long barrel, anyone can shoot. It practically reaches the target with the barrel. No, it's the handgun I can't get to shoot straight."

Emma put her cup down "Will, if you let another lady teacher into your life, I'll teach you all you need to know about hand guns. Okay?"

"If you promise to keep this between us, then I agree, Emma."

"Fine. It's a perfect time to start then. Is there a place I can change my clothes?"

"There's a bedroom at the top of the stairs but the roof's a little low. Will that do?"

"Yep! Down in a minute." She grabbed her bag and went up the stairs.

Ten minutes later she reappeared dressed in a tan, two-piece, close-fitting cowhide outfit. Strapped around her waist was her gun belt with a pistol in both holsters. She stood in front of the men shaking out her long blonde hair.

Both men stood, Masterson in a state of shock. "Miss Emma. My Lord, you are a sight to behold. I . . . I never, well, I . . . never saw a woman . . . what I mean to say, is well . . ."

"It's all right, Will. I know what you mean. You never saw a woman dressed to teach gun lessons. I can't very well teach you while dressed in that long, frilly, wide and dainty skirt, can I?"

Saved, he answered, "No, no I guess not. Sorry."

"Nothing to be sorry about. Do you have a revolver, Will?"

"Yep." He went into his bedroom to a small dresser and took out a pistol, holster and belt. He strapped it on, and they went outside.

The sun was at high noon as she put on her wide-brimmed hat. She set up two-dozen clods of dirt on a fence and paced back one hundred steps. She turned to Masterson and nodded her head toward the targets.

"Will, show me your technique," she said.

He shrugged his shoulders and grinned. He grabbed the revolver, tugged it out of the holster, aimed and pulled the trigger. About thirty feet past the targets, the bullet hit the dirt. He turned toward them. "Told you. I'm really bad."

"True, you need some work, but if you follow my instructions we'll get you there."

Will put his pistol away, kicked some dirt and looked at Bill. "Maybe this project of yours needs someone with quicker reflexes. Maybe I'm not your man, Bill."

"You are the man, Will. If we had someone faster we'd be defeating our project," Bill responded.

Masterson nodded, "Yeah, guess so. I just feel like I'm an impossible student."

Emma put her hand on his shoulder. "Not so, Will. I'll give you some pointers, and you'll see the difference right away."

"If you are the teacher, I'd sure like to have a lesson. Will you give me a demonstration?"

She nodded, turned and faced the targets. "First, always try to have the sun at your back, giving your opponent a disadvantage immediately. Whenever possible, have the wind at your back, too, it helps to keep your opponent squinting into the wind. Another advantage is dirt blowing in their eyes and not yours. When possible, remember the weather of the past day or two. If it was hot with no rain, there's more sand and dirt blowing around than if it had rained recently. Use anything to put your opponent at a disadvantage, even the weather. When you have to shoot it out with someone, shut out all other things around you. Nothing matters except putting the bullet on the target. Nothing! If your opponent is faster than you, then you must be more accurate. Put the bullet where you choose. Watch."

In a blur, Emma's hand whipped out her revolver, aimed and fired six shots. The shots were followed by thuds as the clumps of dry dirt exploded into dust. Both men just stared at her. She walked over to Masterson, undid his gun belt and strapped it on herself. She walked back and faced the targets. Once again her hand flashed and five shots rang out followed by five clumps of dirt disappearing.

Masterson shook his head and said, "Miss Emma, if you think I'll be as quick as you, then you are a miracle worker."

She handed him her gun belt and holster. "Load the revolver and try mine."

He loaded her revolver, put her belt and holsters on and faced the targets. He grabbed the gun and fired three rounds. All three missed. He shrugged his shoulders. "You have your job cut out for you, Emma."

She asked him, "Do you feel the difference between my weapon and yours? Also, the holster?

"Yes. Your holster is lighter than mine. It's easier to take the gun out."

She nodded, "Also, if you notice, I have no sight on the front end of the barrel to snag on the holster as it's being withdrawn. And feel how supple the holster's leather is compared to yours."

Masterson thought a moment and asked, "But don't you need a sight to shoot straight?"

"Why would you need a sight if your opponent is sixty feet away? Nope! It's not needed and just adds a chance of snagging the holster on the way out. We're going to file yours off."

"And the lighter holster? What's the advantage there?" Masterson asked.

"It's not the lightness that makes the advantage. It's lighter because it's made of a thinner cowhide than yours. Thinner and it's oiled to get the suppleness I like. Your holster is designed for carrying your revolver, while mine is designed for quick draw. We're going to go to a boot maker and have him custom-make a holster for you. A holster that will not only carry your revolver, but allow you to draw it out faster than most. Tell me, Will is there a billiards parlor in town?"

He nodded, "Yes, Biffs Pool Hall. They have half a dozen tables. Why?"

"Because that's where you and I are going tonight," Emma said.

"Why? I haven't played a game of billiards in years."

"Were you good when you did play?"

He blushed. "Shucks no! That's why I haven't played lately. Just no darned good at it."

"Well, billiards is a perfect way to improve your hand-eye coordination. Think of the cue stick as the handgun and the white cue ball as the bullet. You look downrange at the target ball and 'shoot' the cue ball to hit the target ball where you want. When we are not practicing with the handgun, we'll be playing billiards. Okay?"

Will smiled and said, "Agreed. You have a funny way of teaching a fellow how to handle a gun, but it sure makes sense."

Bill sat beneath a shade tree as they spoke. He noticed that the two of them were getting comfortable in their roles as teacher and student. He looked at his watch, it was one o'clock. The time traveler lay back and pushed his hat down over his eyes, "Hey, you two. You don't need me, do you? I'm going to take a nap."

The pistol shots quickly become background music as Bill nodded off.

A nudge on his boot woke him. He heard Masterson's voice ask, "Nice nap?" and saw the writer standing over him. The sun was low in the sky.

Bill looked at his pocket watch and exclaimed, "Six-thirty. Boy, I'm hungry."

Emma came out of the house dressed in her skirt and blouse. Masterson exchanged weapons with her. "Talking about being hungry," he said, "do you two have plans for supper tonight? Pearl told me she has a pot roast she's fixing and I'm treating."

Bill got up stiffly. "Fine with me. What about you, Emma?"

She took her gun and holster and offered them to Masterson. "Fine with me, too. Will, why don't I leave my revolver and belt here? We're going to be out here shooting anyway."

"No problem and why not leave your shooting outfit here? Less to carry back and forth." She agreed and later they climbed into the buckboard and drove back to town.

Cleaning up for dinner, Bill carried a pitcher of water to Emma's room and was about to get one for himself when his Time Frequency Modulator gave a low buzz. He opened it, saw he had a text message, and typed in his password.

Bill, hope all is on track. I hate to do this to you in the middle of a mission, but this is urgent. I need you back in New York. I must meet with you. Hopefully, the Roosevelt mission can be held up a few weeks. Text me back as to when we will meet. Edmund Scott, 2066.

Bill read it twice, then knocked on Emma's door. "Emma, it's me, Bill."

"Are you ready, already?' she called out. "I need another fifteen minutes."

"Emma, this is urgent. I have to see you right away." She opened the door and he went in. She was putting her hair up.

"What's wrong?" she asked.

"We have to go back to New York. We have to be on the morning train," he said, with urgency.

"But . . . but . . . the mission. Did I do something wrong?"

He put his hands on her shoulders. "No, no. I just received an urgent text message that the people who send us on these missions need to see me ASAP."

She sat down on the bed. "Damned. And it was going so well. You know, while you were napping, I made some progress with Masterson. He is a fast learner."

Bill shook his head. "What could be so urgent that we have to put off the Roosevelt mission?"

"Why do we have to drop it at all?"

Bill looked at her. "How can we go ahead with it if we have to be in New York for a meeting?"

"Can't you go alone? I mean I'm going to be the one tutoring Masterson anyway?"

Bill's eyebrows raised, "But I can't leave you here alone."

"Why not? I'm a big girl now."

"It's not that, I mean, you are my responsibility."

"I came here of my own free will," she countered, "I think I proved in the club that I fit in. Don't you agree?"

Bill looked at her and exhaled slowly. "Emma, this time period is wild and lawless. Anything can happen."

She countered, "Yes, and anything can happen to the hundreds of other women who live here. I would really love the challenge. And it would validate the existence of the club, would it not?"

After brief consideration, and a walk around the small room, he said, "Well, that *is* the kind of reasoning I used on the past president when I wanted to be alone in New York. It worked then, so . . . " He looked at her. "Why not now? Okay. Let's get this straight. I go back to New York, see what the problem is and you stay here and teach Masterson how to handle his gun."

"Right," she said excitedly.

Bill walked in a circle and said as he rubbed his hands together, "Remember, you must not let him know you are from his future."

"Of course not," she answered. "Then," she continued, "when you are finished with what they want in New York, you can come back and see the progress we've made here. Fair enough?"

Bill nodded. "Fair enough. I'll tell Masterson tonight. Meanwhile, I'm next door. Knock when you are ready."

Back in his room, Bill took the Time Frequency Modulator and typed: *Edmund, It takes about one week to travel from Dodge City to New York. You can expect me around then. I'll text you when I'm there. Regards Bill. PS the Roosevelt project is coming along fine.*

Supper that night was outstanding. Pot roast with mashed sweet potatoes, peas and carrots all smothered in melted butter and beef gravy, and for gravy dipping, as Pearl called it, baked white bread with a thick brown crust. When coffee and apple pie was served, Bill told Masterson his plans.

"Will, I just got a wire that I'm needed back in New York. I'm going to catch the morning train. Emma is going to stay here in Dodge and continue working with you on our project. Is that okay with you?"

Will looked at Emma and said, "Reckon so, Bill. When do you figure you'll be returning?"

"I think in about two weeks. I hope to have to spend only a short time there and hop right back on the train."

Masterson looked at Emma. "I told my editor that my friend and his cousin are in town and I needed some time off. I can take as much as I need. Tomorrow, we can have breakfast, and then shoot some billiards before we go out to my place. If that's all right with you?"

Emma answered, "That'll be fine, Will. Just fine." She turned to Bill and said, "Your project will be going along smoothly, Bill, and you don't have to worry about a thing."

Bill nodded and Masterson spoke up. "I'll keep an eye on your cousin while you are away. So, rest easy, partner."

"I have complete trust in you, Will. Thanks for lightening my load."

The next morning, Bill caught the seven o'clock train going east.

The ride took eight days because a huge herd of Bison decided to graze along the route, and "they just don't respect the train whistle," as the conductor said.

DATELINE: DECEMBER 16, 2011 PLACE: THE 1800 CLUB, NEW YORK CITY

Bill looked forward to a long hot shower in his 2011 apartment as he opened the door. He buzzed Matt, "I'm home, Matt. I'll be in the shower. Will you, please bring me a peanut butter and jelly sandwich and chocolate milk?"

After he had scrubbed the eight days of train dust off, he went into his den and sat at his desk. Matt had brought in his food on a tray, and as Bill attacked it, he sent a text message to the future.

Edmund, I'm back in New York now. Want to chat? Bill.

A return message read.

Welcome home, Bill. Be there in a New York Minute. Edmund.

A knock at the door announced his arrival. Bill opened it and greeted his grandson with a warm hug. He always enjoyed having family around, but this was unique. Bill suggested he take a seat in one of the easy chairs.

Edmund smiled as he sat in the leather easy chair, "So Bill, the Roosevelt mission is moving along fine?"

"Yep. It's a bit more complicated at this moment, but I'm sure it will turn out just the way the history books say it did. Now, what's so important that you dragged me a few thousand miles away?"

Edmund took a deep breath. Bill saw he was having a difficult time with the atmosphere. "Take your time, breathe slowly."

The younger man nodded and took his advice. Finally, he said, "We believe this new trouble could have worse consequences than the trouble with Roosevelt." He paused and took a deep breath.

Bill's eyebrows came together, as he waited for the young man from the future to continue. *Whatever it is,* thought Bill, *it must be bad to pull me back in the middle of a mission.*

Edmund spoke slowly, "One of our probes detected the Wright brothers in 1907 still building bicycles instead of airplanes. We sent probes to other nations and found their airplanes flying while the United States was buying their cast-offs." He paused and took a deep breath before continuing. "We were so far behind that we didn't lead the aviation industry the way history says we did, and the Allies lost World War One."

He wheezed and coughed. "Bill, we have to send you there right away to see what the problem is. According to our computers, the Germans and their allies will occupy Great Britain and France, and the U.S. will have only Canada to trade with. We fear the Germans will attack and win against a weak U.S."

Bill sat back and thought a minute, then turned to Edmund. "Wow! I have to read up on the Wrights and set a plan of action. It'll take me at least one week to learn all I need to know about the brothers, and I'll use that time to finish up the Roosevelt problem. Fair enough?"

"That sounds good to me grandpa . . . uh . . . I mean, Bill. I'm sure the group will be satisfied with that solution."

Edmund looked exhausted and Bill realized that New York City was bathed in fog today and that probably added to his breathing problem.

"Good," he said, "Now, I've got to get you out of here before I lose my future grandson. Next time, why don't you bring an oxygen bottle with you?"

Edmund smiled weakly. "Perhaps I will Bill. Thank you. The group thinks highly of you, and I might add, I'm proud to be your relative."

Bill took his arm and guided him toward the door. "Let's go. And tell them not to worry. Your grandfather will pull it off." He gave Edmund a hug, helped him out, and closed the time portal. That done, Bill finished his sandwich, briefed Matt of his needs for the next day, and went to bed. *I wish they could have just told me the problem rather than having me return to New York. I would have asked them to text me all the information on the Wright brothers that I might need and saved two weeks. Oh well, we're all new at this game.*

He had a train to catch in the morning and he knew what his reading material was going to be: The Wright brothers.

DATELINE: AUGUST 12, 1875, 9:00 A.M. PLACE: DODGE CITY, KANSAS

The train ride back west took five days and Bill spent the time reading up on the Wright brothers and their flying machine. He got off at Dodge City and as usual, there was Timmy looking for a fare. They went to the Splinter and the same clerk napped at his desk. Bill woke him as he dropped his bags.

"Yessir!" he said with a start. "Can I help . . . oh, Mr. Scott, it's you. Do ya' want a room?"

Bill answered as he reached for the pen to sign in, "Yes, of course. Is the same room available? The one next to Miss Walters?"

"Sure is, but Miss Walters isn't here anymore."

Bill was suddenly more alert and leaned toward the clerk. "What do you mean, not here anymore? Where is she?"

The clerk stepped back in fear. "I . . . I . . . I dunno! She left with Mr. Masterson a little over a week ago. She's . . . she's probably shooting billiards with him right now over at Biff's place. They seem to do that a lot. Do . . . do you still want your room?"

Bill looked at his watch. "Yes." He took the key, bounded up the stairs, changed into his black outfit and after getting directions, walked briskly to Biff's billiard hall.

The place was empty. He walked over to the man reading the newspaper behind the counter. He was about to ask of Emma and Masterson when the saloon-style swinging doors opened and they walked in. They were laughing as they went over to the table. Masterson didn't look at the clerk but called to him.

"Biff, rack 'em up for us, would you?" Then Masterson looked up, and he and Emma both saw Bill.

Emma rushed over and embraced him. "Bill! Welcome back. How was it?"

Masterson approached with his hand out, and Bill shook it.

Bill answered, "It was okay. There are still some things I have to take care of in New York, but I have a little time. How come you're not staying at the hotel?"

She blushed. "That creep at the hotel insisted on bringing me water after you left. Then he wanted to bring it into the room and offered to wash my back. I pushed him out. But at night I could hear him sneaking around my door. I told Bat and . . ."

Masterson interrupted, "And I offered to take her in. It made sense. Gets me some more practice time, too. She sleeps upstairs, Bill. There's no messin' on my part."

She blushed again. "Bat's a gentleman, Bill. And what a student! He's got it. That pistol has become part of him."

Bill looked her. "Bat? You said Bat. What's that all about?"

Masterson laughed out loud. "Damned silly, if you ask me. We were in here shooting billiards and three of the boys from town thought they'd get funny with Emma . . ."

Emma cut in, "You should have seen him, Bill. He picked up a cue stick and used it on those three punks. The owner, Biff, started calling him Bat, because he used the stick the way the baseball players use their bats."

"Well, Bat," Bill, said, "do you think we have enough material to write that story?"

Bat looked at him and became serious. "Bill, you were right. After learning how to handle a pistol, doors opened for me. Marshal Earp would like me to be his deputy. It just gave me a new tool to better myself. As I said, it opened more doors for me, but I don't think we should write this story."

Bill looked at him. "Not write it? Why?"

"Because it'd be like telling some young kids that the way to get ahead is to use a gun. And somehow that doesn't seem like the message I want stuck with my name. Do ya' understand, Bill?"

Bill nodded, looked at him and smiled. "Bat Masterson you are one wise man."

"Then you're not angry with me, partner?"

Bill shook his head. "Heck no, Bat, in fact, I'm in awe of you. And I do believe your name will carry a strong message over the years."

Bill looked at Emma. "And you, Emma, do you feel that the project is over?"

"I think that if Bat says it's over, then it's over. And you Bill, what do you think?"

Bat put his cue stick down. "Why don't I let you two cousins talk while I step outside for a spell?" He walked out.

Bill and Emma took a seat in a corner away from the clerk. Bill looked at Emma. She had a deep tan and looked every inch the part of a Western woman, but a very liberated Western woman with her long blond hair flowing freely around her shoulders.

"So, Emma, are you ready to come back home?"

She smiled and shook her head. "No, Bill," she said. "I'm not going back. He's progressed a lot, but he's not ready to be on his own. He needs lots more tutoring. I'm going to stay."

"Stay? For how long?"

"Bill, he asked me to marry him."

Bill's eyes opened wide. "Marry him? You can't marry him!"

Emma put a hand on his shoulder. "Shh, Bill, why can't I marry him? As you said we're here today, alive and breathing. The only difference between us is that I'm from his future. But if I stay here, I become his future."

Bill thought quickly and said, "I don't know if they have a rule against that. I'm, I'm not sure . . ."

Emma opened her hands wide, "Rules? What rules? I'm here, and they're far away. In fact, as you said, they couldn't even come here because of the polluted atmosphere. Do they even know I'm here?"

Bill looked at her, and then broke into a grin. "You know what? I don't think I ever told them that I brought you along." He shrugged his shoulders, "I guess it'd be okay."

She held his hand, "Bill, it's the best thing that could ever happen to me. It's the time period our club members would give anything to live in, and he's so different from any man I've ever met. He's for real! He's an honest, creative man with ideals. I'd be proud to be his wife."

Bat returned and saw them holding hands.

Bill looked up and smiled at the cowboy. "Guess my time here is finished, Bat. I'm going back to New York."

"Think ya' can stay until Saturday?" He put his arm around Emma's waist. "We need a best man at our wedding, and I hoped you would do the honors."

Bill nodded yes, as he saw a tear in Emma's eye, "I'd be proud to, partner."

Saturday was another warm day, and some of the townsfolk tied tumbleweed to the rear of Bat's buckboard. Bill joined in throwing flower seeds at the bride and groom as they drove off.

Emma turned and smiled at him. He waved back. A hand touched his shoulder and he turned to see Wyatt Earp, watching the newly married couple leave town.

"You know, Bill, since you came to town, Will has become a changed man."

Bill smiled at the lawman. "Think so, Wyatt?"

"Yep, partner, I sure do, an' I thank ya." He turned and said as he held his arm out, "If ya have the time, care ta join me in a drink or two?"

"I'd be proud to, partner. I have all the time in the world!"

DATELINE: NOVEMBER 25, 1920 PLACE: BROOKLYN, NEW YORK

It was a snowy night on November 25, 1920. A short, husky man sporting a long white mustache gave a letter to a friend's son.

"Richard," he asked, "will you do me a great favor? I have no kids to do this, so I got to ask that you keep this letter in your family. Pass it down until December 26, 2011, and then have it delivered to the address on the envelope."

The young man took the letter, placed it in a small wall safe and secured it. "I promise Mr. Masterson. It'll be delivered just as you requested."

DATELINE: DECEMBER 26, 2011 PLACE: THE 1800 CLUB, NEW YORK CITY

A young man carrying an envelope rang the doorbell of 520 East Ninth Street, The 1800 Club, and Matt answered the door. The man asked to meet with Bill Scott, the name on the yellowed envelope. Bill was working at his computer when Matt came to his door.

"Sir, a Mr. Caputo is at the door. He has an envelope for you and insists he speak to you only."

Bill pushed away from the computer. "I love a mystery, Matt. Let's go see him." He followed Matt downstairs into the club's den. Bill walked over to the man and offered his hand. "I'm Bill Scott. I understand you have some mail for me, sir?"

The man shook his hand. "I'm Richard Caputo. I live about thirty blocks from here." He showed Bill the old envelope. "This envelope has been in my family since 1920. A friend of my grandfathers gave it to him with instructions that it is delivered today. I don't know what it's about, but it's been the talk of my family for years and I'm here to fulfill the man's wish."

Bill took it and walked over to a small table, sat and opened it. In neat handwriting it read, "Bill, if you get this letter, please come to 570 Tenth Street, Brooklyn, New York, on November 25, 1920 after eight P.M. Regards, your friend, Will "Bat" Masterson."

Bill looked up and shook his head. Caputo was still there. *He deserves an answer after all these years,* Bill thought.

"Mr. Caputo, this is a letter from an old friend of the family. It's sort of a time capsule saying hello to the future Scotts. Thank you so much. Could I give you some good Cuban cigars for your family's stewardship of the letter all these years?"

Caputo smiled. "I wasn't here for a reward, Mr. Scott, just honoring an old family wish. However, I'd enjoy a good cigar."

Bill turned to Matt and said, "Matt, please get Mr. Caputo a dozen Cubans from my private stock." Then he offered his hand to his visitor. "Thank you again, Mr. Caputo. Wait here and Matt will be right back."

Bill walked quickly back to his den and reread the letter. *Got to honor it,* he thought, as he changed into 1920s clothes. He took some 1920's currency, dialed the Time Frequency Modulator to November 25, 1920, and went out the door.

DATELINE: NOVEMBER 25, 1920, 7:00 P.M. PLACE: THE 1800 CLUB'S GARDEN, NEW YORK

The time traveler walked through the garden and out into the New York of 1920. It started to snow and he pulled the long black overcoat tight to him as he walked over to Broadway. Sparks flew from the overhead wires as an electric trolley car stopped at his corner. Bill got in and stayed on until he reached downtown and the Brooklyn Bridge. At the last stop, he caught a yellow taxi over it. *A drafty taxi,* he thought as it went over the bridge, slipping on the wet, steel-mesh flooring high above the cold, windblown waters. The snow started to fall heavily and the cab's wipers were having a hard time pushing the large, wet snowflakes away.

Once on the Brooklyn side, he directed the driver toward Prospect Park. From there, they went to Tenth Street and Seventh Avenue. He asked the man to wait, and then walked up the block to 570, the address on the envelope. The sidewalk's gray, slate slabs were slippery with the snow that was now sticking to them and Bill treaded carefully as he looked at the row houses for his destination.

The dim light cast by the early streetlight showed the numbers 570 painted on the steps leading into one of the turn-of-the-century row houses. In the vestibule of the three-story building, he saw mailboxes fitted into the wall. Bill lit a small flashlight and spotted the name he wanted on the first floor. There was no bell, so he entered, walked down a short, hallway that a gaslight fought to push back the darkness and rapped lightly on the door. There was a shuffling on the other side, and then it opened.

Bill immediately recognized him, though forty of his years had passed. His hair was just as long, but pure white, as was his mustache and he squinted through glasses. The time traveler smiled and offered his hand. The man shook it, and then both embraced as Bill said, "Bat Masterson, how the heck are you?"

"Just fine, Bill, just fine. Come on in." He held the door and Bill walked into a small hall leading to a well-lit kitchen. Bat closed the door and escorted him into a sitting room.

"Sit, Bill. Somethin' ta drink? Coffee, Scotch, beer? What's your poison, old friend?"

"Whatever you're having, Bat."

"Two beers it is." He walked to the kitchen, opened the icebox, took out a quart bottle of beer and poured two glasses. Bat came back into the living room with the two tall glasses of beer, handed one to Bill, and then raised his in a toast. "To old friends and old times."

Bill raised his glass, "Old friends and old times."

They both drank then Bat looked at Bill and smiled, "Old, applies to only one of us in this case, though."

"What made you send the message to me, Bat?"

"Ingenious, right?"

Bill nodded, "Damned ingenious." He looked around, "Emma? Is she all right?"

"She's fine, Bill. Just fine . . . for an old woman. And that's the reason I asked you to come here. She's at her friend's house, playing cards, so we can talk man to man." He took a long drink and gave Bill a serious look. "Bill, you knew when you received my letter that I knew all about you and Emma time traveling."

Bill nodded. "I figured Emma had told you everything."

"She did. She's a fine woman, Bill, and she did her job well. She told me when to write a letter to Roosevelt and just what to say. He and I became pretty good friends over the years. And from what I understand, the time problem has fixed itself. Am I right?"

"It did, Bat. It worked just as we hoped."

"It worked because of a great woman, Bill, Emma Walters, my wife. She saved the future. Now I have a favor to ask."

"Whatever I can do for you two, Bat, name it."

"Take her back."

Bill did a double take. "Take her back? I don't understand."

Bat swiped the froth from his mustache. "Bill, as you can see we are old now, and you're still a youngster. I figure you can take her back home from, say, 1900. The future would have been set by then, and she wouldn't have to spend her whole life here. Take her back so she can be young again."

"Did she ask for this, Bat?"

"Heck no. It's me asking for it. I'm a grouch, and she doesn't need to be strapped to me . . . not when she can get out and be that pretty lady I married when we were young."

There was a movement in the entrance to the living room. Both men turned and saw Emma standing there as she removed her scarf.

Damn! She's still a handsome woman, Bill thought, as he stood up.

She smiled at him and they embraced. "Bill Scott! You son-of-a-gun! You are a sight for old eyes. Isn't he, Bat? A sight for *old* eyes." She emphasized the word "old."

She walked over and sat on the armrest of Bat's easy chair and hugged him. "Claire wasn't feeling up to cards, so I came home early." She looked at the old cowboy. "Bat, I heard every word you said and want you to remember the words, 'Till death do us part.' Do you think I'd let Bill take me away from you? Never! I stayed here on my own, not to just finish some silly project. That became secondary very soon after I met you, Bat Masterson."

Bat looked sheepishly at her. "But, Em, you can go back and be young again. I can handle it."

She kissed the top of his head, "But *I* couldn't. No, cowboy, we are in the long cattle drive together, so you have to get used to it."

He kissed her hand.

Bill finished his drink. "Is there anything I can do for you two?"

Emma laughed. "You can get the heck out of here so we can go to bed. Lord, it's after nine, and we need our beauty rest."

Bill smiled. "Neither of you need any beauty rest. You're two of the most beautiful people I've ever met."

They all rose and hugged one another. Bill walked to the door, hesitated and turned around. "Emma, you did a great job. If you two ever need me, just send a message up."

She smiled and waved as she held Bat's hand.

Bill walked out the door and into the snowy night. By the time he reached the corner, the white powder had covered his footprints erasing all traces of his presence. He took a cab back to New York City and the 1800 Club.

AUTHOR'S NOTE:

The end is usually very apparent in a story, be it a book or movie. However, in this case, although it is the end page-wise, it continues on in The 1800 Club. You see, The 1800 Club *does* exist in New York City, though, under a different name and address. I,

Bill Scott, also exist as President and owner of the club, and the people I wrote of, all exist. Some of their names have been changed, as they do have a life outside of the club, and they and the club must be protected.

By now you are thinking, "This is a put-on, there is no club that can travel in time." But, I ask you to look around. Isn't history the same as you read it in your history books? Believe me the club is working to keep it so. You the reader may ask, "Why is he admitting this?" To that I answer, "Why not?" Sometimes the best place to hide something is right out in plain sight! So, while admitting the club exists, the secret is as safe as saying it doesn't exist.

I intended to continue this narrative and tell you about some of the other missions the club has worked on, however, I have to interrupt this book at this point because I've just been alerted that there is a problem going on right now with the Wright brothers. I do intend to document it and others as they occur, in the next book, *'Time Travel Adventures of The 1800 Club. Book 2.'*

B.S.

Note from Robert P. McAuley

After each adventure in time, President Bill Scott dictates to me what occurred so I can write them down for posterity. He told me that at this moment there are thirty plus stories on hand and, as time goes on, who knows how many more there will be after that? He informed me that I might let our readers know that ***Book II*** will feature two more stories: ***The Time Travel Adventure To Help The Wright Brothers Fly*** *and* **The Problem With The Hindenburg Exploding Over The Ocean.** We both hope you find the time to read them. The following is the opening of **The Wright Brother's Problem**

Regards, Robert P. McAuley

The Wright Brothers Problem

DATELINE: JULY 6, 1907 PLACE: DAYTON, OHIO

On a warm summer evening, a butterfly fluttered gently across a garden lush with summer greenery and alighted on a swing that hung on a small white porch. It shared the wooden porch with three men and a woman. Warm light from the house's living room spilled onto the porch's floor and the butterfly watched as one of the men, who was short and bald, got up and poured lemonade for the four of them. He put the pitcher down and joined the others as they looked up at the stars. He sighed and said, "It's a beautiful evening, isn't it?"

The woman answered for them all. "Yes, a wonderful way to end a nice weekend. Family, friends, lemonade and the stars shining brightly in the sky."

The screen door opened and a small, elderly man put his head out and said, "Good night, children. Good night, Mr. Osloe."

Two of the men answered in unison, "Good night, father."

From the doorway, the man wagged a finger at his two sons. "Orville, Wilbur, don't forget you have to finish Reverend Pots' bicycle tomorrow. I gave him my word at this morning's service."

The young, dark-haired woman went over and kissed him on the cheek. "Good night, Father. I won't be late."

One of the men turned to the other and said, "Orville, how much time do you figure it'll take to finish the reverend's bicycle?"

The tall, balding man looked up at the stars again, thought and answered, "Should be finished and ready for a test ride by lunchtime."

The third man on the porch was short at only five feet tall, and as he stood next to the brothers, he made them look even taller than their six-foot height. He smiled at the woman and spoke quietly as he held up his empty glass. "Miss Katharine, may I have some more lemonade?"

She brushed back a wisp of hair from her face and reached for his empty glass. "Of course, Mr. Osloe. Did you enjoy it?"

He smiled as he wiped his baldhead. "I do enjoy it, and I find it keeps me cool."

Both men smiled at the man.

"Do they not have lemonade in your native land, Mr. Osloe?" asked Wilbur.

He sipped the frosty drink and said, "Not as tangy, Wilbur. I find this lemonade very agreeable."

When they were finished, Katharine picked up the empty glasses and put them on a tray along with the pitcher. "Good night, gentlemen," she said. She walked toward the door as Wilbur held it open for her. He pecked her cheek.

"Good night, sweet sister. See you for breakfast."

She looked back through the screen door, "Good night, Orville. And you boys remember what Father said. He gave his word."

At that moment, a streak of light flew across the sky, and the brothers became visibly excited.

"Wilbur! Did you see that? A shooting star!" Both scanned the heavens.

Wilbur responded, "Yes! Yes! It was a shooting star, and there could be more. Remember the night we counted three in one hour?"

"Yes," Orville answered, "that was a wonderful evening. I propose we stay up a little later and watch. Mr. Osloe, will you watch with us?"

The little man smiled and joined them on the top wooden step.

"Yes, my friends, I would enjoy that very much."

Orville kept his eyes on the sky as he said to his brother, "To fly, Wilbur, to fly. Would that not be great?"

"Yes," said his sibling, "and we got so close, then . . . well . . ."

Orville looked at his brother and patted his arm. "Don't fret, brother. We'll get it right soon. Watch and see. Right, Mr. Osloe?"

Their guest nodded. And the butterfly-probe flew off into the night.

DATELINE: 2066 PLACE: HISTORY TRACKING CENTER, NEW YORK CITY

Alexis Shuntly ran the meeting. She stood at the head of a long, highly polished mahogany table. Seated around it were the other members of the History Watchers Group, four men and a woman. They stared at a hologram in the middle of the table and the scene that was unfolding. The realistic moving pictures were the product of the Time Probing Butterfly robot that now sat on a shelf with other probes. After some minutes in which no one spoke, Alexis sat down and looked around at her colleagues through her thick glasses.

She squinted and said, "It's 1907. They were supposed to be flying in December of 1903. What could have gone wrong?"

John Hyder, seated on her right, asked, "Did we get the

computer projections on this? How bad is it if they aren't the inventors of flight?"

"They were not the inventors of flight," said a woman's voice. All eyes focused on Maryellen Muldey, seated across from Hyder.

"They didn't invent flight. What they did was become the first to fly a heavier-than-air machine that had direction controllability. They were the first to be able to fly in any direction they wanted."

Alexis Shuntly opened a notebook and looked at Hyder. "The computer projects that the French became the first to have controlled flight. They were content to just fly about and sell their aircraft to other countries. The British were broke with the recession and didn't see the need for aviation. History shows that an American, Bill Cody, was the first to fly in England and that influenced them to push aviation forward. But if the Wright brothers hadn't shown the way, Cody wouldn't have gotten into flying, and the Brits wouldn't have been ready for World War One." She paused to let that sink in, and then continued in a low voice.

"The Germans, on the other hand, would have put their money and resources into the aircraft Anthony Fokker was designing. He had some real winners and once World War One started, the Germans and their allies would have been unstoppable. France would have fallen and the Germans would have invaded and occupied Britain. The Americas, too, would have been targets."

She put down the notebook and looked at the others. "Dear friends and fellow History Watchers, if this is not corrected, we are all in great danger. Not just us but the world as we know it today. I don't know why the Wright brothers didn't make that historic flight, but it has to be remedied. Do we all agree that we must send someone back and guide the brothers? May I see a show of hands for a trip?"

Every hand was raised in agreement. Alexis pressed a button, the door opened and a tall man entered carrying a small notebook. He smiled at them and said, "You rang, Miss Shuntly?"

Alexis nodded. "Yes, Ted. We need a Time Trip back to 1903." She held up a hand and said, "Wait, no, make that 1902." She glanced at the others. "If they achieved their first flight in 1903, what year would they have started? I mean, when would they have first shown interest in flight?"

Maryellen Muldey looked up from her laptop computer and said, "They were making toy helicopters when they were little boys, but they started flying large gliders in 1900 at Kitty Hawk, North Carolina. I think our traveler would have to be present about 1901." Murmurs of approval came from around the table.

Alexis ran her fingers through her short, brown hair and sighed. "Fine then," she said and turned to give instructions to the young man. "Ted, will you contact our liaison to the head of The 1800 Club who handles that time period and set it up?"

Ted consulted his notebook, then looked at her and said, "That'd be Edmund Scott from our time period contacting Bill Scott of the 2011 period."

She looked at the others and seeing no disagreement, said to him, "Fine. Will you set up a meeting with Edmund Scott as soon as possible? I'll brief him on the situation."

She stood, and the meeting was over.

Read the Wright Brother's Mission in Book 2

Other books by Robert P. McAuley

Sky Ship
Romance in a Ghost Town
Vampire's Bloodline
Aviation, Facts & Rumors Book 1
Aviation, Facts & Rumors Book II
The Dripping Sands Of Time
A New Jersey Yankee In King Arthur's Court
Time Travel Adventures of The 1800 Club: Book 1
Time Travel Adventures of The 1800 Club: Book 2
Time Travel Adventures of The 1800 Club: Book 3
Time Travel Adventures of The 1800 Club: Book 4
Time Travel Adventures of The 1800 Club: Book 5
Time Travel Adventures of The 1800 Club: Book 6
Time Travel Adventures of The 1800 Club: Book 7
Time Travel Adventures of The 1800 Club: Book 8
Time Travel Adventures of The 1800 Club: Book 9
Time Travel Adventures of The 1800 Club: Book 10

Printed in Great Britain
by Amazon

87377084R00150